TANGENT
TANGENT
GENTS

Right: Tower Bridge from the Tower of London terrace
Following page: sculptural group by Carpeaux on the south front of the Paris Opera

Dedication

To my wife, my partners and my friends

THE NECESSARY MONUMENT

Theo Crosby

Studio Vista London

Published in Great Britain by Studio Vista Limited
Blue Star House, Highgate Hill, London N19
Set in 9/11 Univers 689
Printed in Great Britain by Fletcher and Son Ltd, Norwich
Bound by Richard Clay Ltd, Bungay, Suffolk

SBN 289 79765 9 (paper)
289 79775 6 (hardback)

Contents

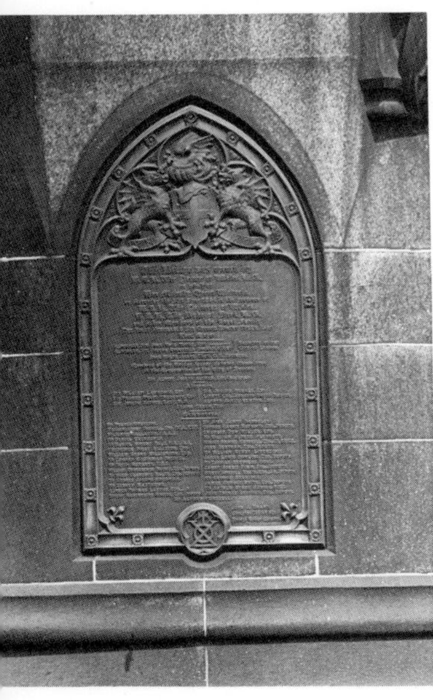

Above and below: memorial plaque on the southern approach of Tower Bridge

Preface

Most members of my generation were weaned on the 'modern movement' and the past was interpreted for us by a generation of critics (Roger Fry, Sigfried Giedion, Nikolaus Pevsner, J. M. Richards), as a sometimes wayward but always inevitable preparation for our own revolutionary era. In effect, history was used highly selectively to justify the present and to promote a whole series of attitudes which seemed essential and inevitable.

The 'movement' was born in the early years of the century, at the moment when it became apparent that technology was entering a new phase: mass production. The possibilities of this new world of motor vehicles and flight, of radio and electric light were seen to be enormous, and marvellously liberating. In the arts, however, the problems of mass production had been a constant threat through most of the nineteenth century. Artists had welcomed and pioneered photography and within sixty years had seen their main source of income (the creation and control of images) disappear. From being a central, primary factor in society, the artist became a bohemian, a worker at the fringe.

This same process is now undermining the profession of the architect. Industrialization of building has come late to full mechanization, but the process will as surely make the concept of the architect as a form giver obsolete.

It has been pointed out that to achieve the maximum benefits of technology there has to be a continuous adaptation by society to the requirements of the technology. In particular, the intellectual and creative elements in society must be bent to the service of the machine. And to serve well, they must learn to love it.

This subservience has been so gradual and is now so complete as to be almost unconscious. The interdependence of the industrial state and the intellectual community has effects far outside the simple matter of providing technicians for the corporations, or grants for the study of potentially useful weaponry. It reaches into every minute part of our lives, altering our modes of perception and conditioning our understanding. Thus we learn to love frozen peas, because ordinary peas are quite simply not there. The taste of the natural vegetable is the merest memory. On the other hand we have a wide choice of equally frozen alternatives.

The same accommodation has been reached in the environmental sense. It is convenient for our miserably inept building industry to cover large areas with repetitive blocks of identical dwellings; at the same time this dehumanizing environment is accepted as socially good, because the system produces the maximum number of minimum homes for the least apparent cost. It has been, and is, accepted as inevitable.

Above: a Victorian building in the City of London which manages to retain a civilized scale and architectural complexity in the midst of barbarian redevelopment

In such a world, the past is an embarrassment. Old buildings are therefore considered pretentious and over decorated. It is no accident that the plainest style, the neo-classic or Georgian, has been the most esteemed for sixty years. Buildings with more content, the Baroque or late Victorian, have few friends.

Yet it is precisely this embarrassment that we should now begin to probe and understand, and to resolve, because it provides a key to our relation to the past and to the present. It may show a possible way out of our own impasse in relation to the machine. In our cities the monuments of the nineteenth century provide an abrasive element which our culture has as yet been unable to assimilate. Above all, they are enormous *examples* of an alternative mode of perception, of another set of priorities, an alternative to our accommodation to the industrial system.

The effect of this intellectual accommodation and acquiescence is now very obvious all around us. Cities once beautiful are now accepted as 'spoiled', and no-one quite knows why, though they tend to blame the planners.

One may as well blame the police for crime.

The necessary monument

The image of a city is made up of its landmarks, its monuments, and this book is an attempt to evaluate the role of the 'spectacular' building in several ways. In particular, there is the question of how far the purely economic role of a building can, or should be, subsumed by its other life as a spectacle; and also what is to be done with it when its primary function has been completed, and it has to subsist on its secondary roles.

This latter is a condition now affecting most of the great, apparently functional, buildings of the nineteenth century. Because of their commercial origins, they are subject to economic pressures and changes of use, which work against the automatic preservation accorded to more ancient monuments. Our society is as yet unwilling to support them entirely for their visual qualities, and at the same time cannot bring itself to allow them to be unceremoniously replaced.

The purely economic argument has the merits of simplicity: a building represents a certain capital outlay, from which a return can be expected for a specific period, as with any other investment. After the period has elapsed, the value has been earned and theoretically it would be logical and profitable to replace it with a new building, which would in turn be treated in the same way. Our cities would therefore go through continuous cycles of rebuilding, at progressively shorter intervals as our capital formation capacity grows with our technology.

There are, in fact, many areas of the world where this elementary system is in operation, but when looked at closely, it is not really very simple at all. Firstly, those cities which have a rapid renewal rate are always very new, pioneering settlements such as Sydney, Johannesburg or Los Angeles, caught in a vast population growth and a simultaneous increase in productivity. Their rapid turnover is due mainly to rising site values. If the land becomes more valuable than the buildings on it, a change becomes an economic necessity.

In societies where economic factors are allowed full play (once again in newly established, pioneering societies), the problem of the necessary but unwanted building does not arise, and in any case there are, by the very nature of the place, few such buildings.

In the maturely grown city, with a vast accumulation of structures, however, the problem is quite different, and the economics, like everything else, are no longer simple. A vast number of complicating factors have arisen, owing to the human activity in the years since the building was built; a million individual decisions have affected the building, the site and the neighbourhood. Values have risen or dropped, and above all, the community itself has become involved in decisions once left to the individual developer.

In the past twenty years the planner, as the agent of community involvement, has appeared on the scene, full of theories, in their own way often as simplistic as those of the nineteenth-century economists. His intervention in the environment has been almost uniformly deadening. Our surroundings are today in many respects infinitely worse than those of 150 years ago. Compared to the complex social and economic mechanisms of Nash's Regent's Park in London, a new town is as elementary as a box of children's blocks, and about as satisfactory to live in.

Yet our lives are infinitely more complicated than in 1820. Distance and time hold few terrors for us. We move easily all over the world, know a great deal of all cultures living and dead. Above all, there are so many more of us, all communicating as hard as we can. Our culture is a labyrinth, a vast storehouse of treasures instantly available; yet we live in miserable little boxes and in a growing squalor.

A fantastic contradiction.

We need to begin to look for a theory (for a theory is always necessary and without one no decision can ever be justified), which will allow us to build the correct environment without shame or guilt. This theory will have to accommodate a whole string of apparently contradictory factors, economic, social and political; it will have to work in the short as well as long terms. It will need to be able to deal with wholes within which parts can be integrated.

Planning ideas are now in considerable disarray. The increasing pressures of technology (mobility and mass production are the two aspects of technology which immediately affect environment) have created almost automatically a social and physical form which can be summed up in the words 'Los Angeles': the city, or non-city, of sprawling suburbs held together by super-highways; a way of life conditioned by the car, for transportation, and television, for entertainment. Both inventions create and sustain individual and family isolation at the environmental level while providing a compensatory shadow participation in the macro-world. Thus total awareness of world events coexists with total ignorance of even one's immediate surroundings. At the same time there is an appalled realization that we have unwittingly lost irreplaceable treasures, discarded irrecoverable aesthetic and social pleasures for the benefits of an ephemeral technology.

The theories on which modern planning is based are descended from the preoccupation with public health in the nineteenth century. They are basically preventive, and negative. The modern movement in architecture brought to this body of expertise a concern for logic, for precision and for equality that fitted precisely with the technological and social preoccupations of the 'twenties. In those early days of mass production the processes of manufacture were continually subdivided, and simplified: 'piece-work', a very revealing definition. This organizational technique, applied to cities, produces a set of tests and rules for new buildings: light angles, plot ratios, density allowances, zoning areas, added to the existing sanitary regulations. The resulting product, like the equivalent end result of early mechanization in other fields, was an introvert and hermetic object, economically and structurally self-sufficient, and of course, inevitably, architecturally independent and self-regarding. The ideal city image was a collection of buildings camping in a public park. Every element in the problem that the planner, the developer or the architect could control was pushed toward this technical solution; and none could foresee the social and aesthetic cost that would have to be paid.

This account must now be settled. We find ourselves in cities almost destroyed by our own adherence to such primitive logic. Technology has moved on and is now quite unconcerned with products any more. It is now concerned with systems, with processes, with connections between processes. A new generation of planning theorists is not far behind, adapting the methodology and computer games, with equally little concern for things felt and seen, or for the users who have to live and work in the resulting environment.

In this flux of theoretical change, and with the humbling example of our theories being demonstrated (in a very short space of time) to be thoroughly inadequate, we must realistically hang on to what we have, and try to perceive its value. Propagandists of modern architecture rewrote history to prove the inadequacy of our predecessors, choosing a line of development that would lead logically to our revered pioneers – Gropius, le Corbusier and Mies van der Rohe – and denigrating those who would not fit the theory. Thus we withdrew intellectual support from the non-conforming architects of the past, and made no protest when their buildings were threatened or butchered, or when architecturally unfashionable areas were 'redeveloped'. Once a pattern of disrespect is established it is very difficult to eradicate, as we can also observe in many other fields.

Our pervasive communications system, too, works against us in many subtle ways. Theory, opinion and controversy are circulated rapidly and widely from the centres where controversy seems to originate, a few great cities. In the context of these cities the opposition, and stability, of the intellectual audience provides a damping effect, and nothing drastic seems to happen. The argument is simply part of the game of city life. In areas of less dense intellectual involvement, however, the effect is to cancel out existing opinion, and promote intellectual insecurity. An example: the development of the Costa Brava in Spain, where an international commercial modernism has undermined and destroyed a perfectly adequate provincial tradition of building, in itself a major attraction of the area.

In places without tradition, but with a dynamic economy, such as Los Angeles, any innovation or new ideology is acceptable, and technology runs free, to establish the natural form of the corporate society. There is nothing to lose, and perhaps something dramatic to gain. Such is not the case in mature cities, where technology can be recognized as only one of many shaping forces. Here the existing structures, whether intellectual, physical, social or economic, are more able to resist or to incorporate radical concepts.

'An architecture of our time' has always been a radical concept. To promote it now requires a realization that, after sixty years of pioneering, we must take a wider, more inclusive view, to test the present in the context of the past as well as the hopeful future.

This book is an attempt to follow a single thread towards a new method of looking at and dealing with cities. It tries to isolate a single element in the marvellously complex fabric and to *see* it; and to share the enormous pleasure of discovery. It is not original; it is not inventive; our awakening to the importance of nineteenth-century architecture has been initiated by Nikolaus Pevsner, and many others less persuasive; the social consequences of technology on cities have been explored by Jane Jacobs and William H. Whyte, to whose works I owe a great deal.

POESIE LYRIQUE
SIQUE
HALEVY

The Paris Opéra: a monument reborn

When General de Gaulle came to power in 1959 France was deeply divided, sapped by long and pointless wars in Vietnam and Algeria, and technologically backward. De Gaulle's strategy of renouncing the French Empire and concentrating on building a powerful and independent nation has proved masterly. By lavish expenditure on the newest technologies he changed the direction of the economy. Very soon this investment began to pay off in terms of Mirage bombers and nuclear power, but also – more importantly – in the creation of the technostructure which organizes and produces these things. In a remarkably short time France closed the technological gap. The roads, however energetically rebuilt, cannot today contain the vast numbers of cars; the cities are crammed with countrymen seeking the affluent life; computer programmers lurk at every corner.

Within five years de Gaulle had changed the spirit of his country from anxiety and depression, to security and confidence. In fact, the imposition of the new problems of affluence on the volatile and intelligent French brought inevitably the crisis of conscience of the student uprisings, and the equally predictable indifference of the workers. In the crises of mature capitalism, idealist youth sides with the underprivileged; the well-paid worker identifies with the technostructure.

Within the strategy to contain the larger social problems, however, de Gaulle produced a host of intelligent tactics to focus the attention of his countrymen on the building and renovation of France. Apart from expenditure on technology (dams, nuclear power stations, a rocket programme, atomic submarines and the usual defence apparatus of the advanced countries) there are in hand enormous programmes for regional transformation, new towns, and above all, the restructuring of Paris.

No country is so focused on its capital as France. Here are the schools, the institutes, the concentrated apparatus of government. Above all, Paris is the symbol of France. The decision to clean the buildings of the capital was simple, brave and intelligent. It was such a direct and obvious thing to do, but it went against a century of traditional grubbiness, when to paint your mansion was to invite a visit from the tax man. The government set an example, cleaning its own buildings, including the churches which had been nationalized in 1790. Area by area the city has been cleansed, individual owners persuaded, bribed or threatened into conformity.

Left: east pavilion of the south front of the Opéra. Note the effortless integration of diverse and complex elements of architecture and sculpture

The results are nothing short of miraculous. Paris is revealed as the most beautiful city in the world.

At the same time programmes for the conservation of historic areas

The Paris Opéra: a monument reborn

The Paris Opéra: a monument reborn

were set in motion, in Paris and other cities. In Paris the Marais, the seventeenth-century area around the Place des Vosges, is being quietly renovated, the palaces restored and converted to flats and appartments.

Initially the money for conservation comes from the state, through a characteristic maze of quasi-public corporations which also involves banks and building societies. Since the consequences of sustained investment have become apparent, private money has flooded in. The Marais has become fashionable, and the state and its partners have an excellent investment.

Part of the first phase of the cleaning programme were the great monuments: the Louvre, Notre Dame, the Madeleine and the Opéra. Each is revealed as an architectural miracle which our generation is privileged to see as no one has seen them for a century. Of these the most surprising is the Opéra.

The Nouvel Opéra de Paris was the greatest work of Charles Garnier, whose bust stands outside the west door. It is perhaps the prototypical academic building. Precisely within the main tradition of the Ecole des Beaux-Arts, it gave that tradition a powerful impetus and ensured the dominance of French classicism

Right: general view and left, a detail from the south front

The Paris Opéra: a monument reborn

for fifty years. Jean-Louis Charles Garnier* was born in 1825 and was a student of Levéil, Lebas and the Ecole des Beaux-Arts. At the Ecole he won the Grand Prix de Rome in architecture in 1848, and spent his years at the French Academy in Rome measuring Roman remains and Renaissance monuments. At this time the sixth-century temple of Zeus at Aegina was discovered. It was remarkably complete, retaining much of its polychromy, and Garnier produced the influential publication drawings. After journeys to Constantinople and Sicily he returned to Paris, to work for the department of public works. Always a superb draughtsman, his professional debut was to win, at the age of thirty-six, the competition for the Opéra, against 171 competitors in the first stage and four others in the second.

* Garnier's subsequent works included the Casino at Monte Carlo, the church and school at Bordighera, the Casino, baths, and hotel at Vittel, numerous villas, the tombs of Bizet, Offenbach and Victor Masse. At the Paris Exposition of 1889 he was the consulting architect. He died in 1898 loaded with honours: member of the Institut de France, Grand Officer of the Legion of Honour, RIBA Royal Gold Medallist etc., etc.

Above: the gilt bronze bust of Garnier outside the west carriage entrance
Left and right: details of the south front

The Paris Opéra: a monument reborn

The Paris Opéra: a monument reborn

The new building was destined to fill a space that had been painstakingly prepared by Rouhalt de Fleury and Henri Blondel in 1858. The Place de l'Opéra is remarkably plain and severe, in the coldest neo-classic style, and the surrounding palaces perfectly contrast with the exuberant polychromy and formal complexity of Garnier's building. The Opéra is in many ways curiously un-French and was much maligned at the time of its construction. It was considered squat, vulgar and garish, though everyone accepted its powerful imagery and recognized its virtues. Even today the building comes as a shock. Blinded by familiarity with all the world's buildings as we are, we can never recapture the impact that this great building had when it was opened in January 1875, fourteen years after the first stones were laid. Though the building was virtually finished in 1870, the Franco-Prussian war delayed completion. Ironically, the building most associated with the style of Napoleon III was never visited by the Emperor.

Left: the main public entrance. Garnier designed or supervised the superb bronze lamps, railings and other decorative elements which complement the building
Below: the Opéra circa 1908

The Paris Opéra: a monument reborn

Above: the salon over the east entrance

Left: the east carriageway entrance

Below left: detail of the south front

Below: the shadowed north front

The style is more Italian than French, in its rich modelling and in its three-dimensional plasticity. The way Garnier used arcades, through which vistas and further architectural elements can be seen, owed much to Piranesi; and the whole splendid tumbling edifice is massed, with contrasting volumes starting from the arcaded façade, through the dome of the auditorium to the tall scenery tower, with a Baroque exuberance. The order and clarity of its organization is best appreciated on the plan. In walking around the building one is more conscious of the sculptural control, the rich plasticity of the façades, and the sheer invention of the detailing. It is not archaeological. In the spiky forms which contrast with the classical mouldings, there is more than an echo of the Art Nouveau which was to come in the 'nineties. Each front has its major feature which draws the eye: the south entrance is arcaded and richly shadowed, dominating the immense Avenue de l'Opéra cut through to the Louvre in 1878. The west front is pompous with ramped carriageways for the Emperor's coach. Here the decoration takes on an added luxuriance: caryatides and eagles abound, all freely articulated within a tight architectural control. The north front is flat, shadowed and gloomily impressive and the east has another important entrance under a dome.

The Paris Opéra: a monument reborn

Above and right: details of one of the bronze lights, a perfect example of Second Empire style
Left: details of the entrance on the west front; the sheer virtuousity of the carving is breathtaking

Following pages: cross section and elevation of the Opéra, from the publication drawings which are perhaps the finest ever produced for any building

Coupe sur la Salle

The Paris Opéra: a monument reborn

Above, below and left: the Grand Escalier d'Honneur

Below right: a ceiling boss in the entrance hall

The interior is a brilliant sequence of extraordinarily complex spaces, interpenetrating each other, offering galleries, stairs and promenades to see and to be seen. The spectators are all actors in a stage set where everyone plays his most elegant role.

The interior decoration is incredibly rich and complex, and always inventive. Throughout the building one feels the presence of painters and sculptors. Their work (capitals, murals, complex mouldings, mosaic floors and sculptural groups) organized and systematized by the architect, adds to but is not dominated by the architecture. Such an integration of the arts, possible within a coherent aesthetic philosophy such as that of the Beaux-Arts, seems incredible today. To come upon such a richly worked example is an experience which produces, in the end, despair. In our time the early hopes of the integration of painting and sculpture into modern architecture have come to grief on the commercial gallery system with its premium on artistic individuality and extremism on one side, and the pressures of economy and technology on the other.

In the Opéra the technologies of the arts are still in balance, the materials of the artist the same as those of the builder, only richer and more concentrated. Decoration then was not a dirty word. Thus the sculptural groups by Carpeaux, outward going and energetic, are symbolic, in subject and material, of the intention of the building as a whole. It is just this coherence that makes the building particularly valuable, that makes it such a lesson to our fragmented aesthetic. The Opéra stands near the end of an epoch, and incorporates the hard won lessons of 400 years. It is obvious that to achieve a similar wholeness we have to correct many basic tendencies in our culture. This will take time, and perhaps a good deal of blood and tears, but the example of a great extrovert building is highly relevant to the future form of cities.

A monument in balance: Tower Bridge

A monument in balance: Tower Bridge

Tower Bridge is a building that produces an effect on its surroundings infinitely greater than its elemental function as a traffic machine. This is due to its size, and to its complexity as a mechanism, as an element of urban enclosure and as an historical commentary.

It is a large bridge, 142 feet high, literally closing the river from both directions with a web of granite and steel. Without its vertical scale, it could not relate the two river banks to form one of the largest open spaces in London, the Pool. Though the south bank is now greatly decayed, this great enclosure is a model for a city space, filled with incident, with cranes and ships, with a back-ground of glowering warehouses on the south and a sunlit north bank full of splendid buildings: Adelaide House; Wren's St Magnus the Martyr, the Customs House, and above all, the Tower. In this context the bridge far exceeds its function, and becomes an architectural dominant.

Much of its success arises from its intrinsic complexity as a mechanism. Because the roadway must rise to allow for the passage of ocean-going ships, the physical problems within the structure are enormous. Their detailed solution, one of the great triumphs of Victorian engineering, is described in the appendix. Within the context of the city, however, this complexity of use provides the programme for a unique building: a road capable of movement, machine rooms, control offices, living quarters for a working community. In comparison, the simplistic briefs given to the engineers of contemporary motorways are elementary. Because their programmes are elementary, the final results are always dull.

The bridge is in high Victorian Gothic, and stylistically responds to the mediaeval Tower, and self-righteously comments upon it. The sharp, hard, granite detailing mocks the latter's crumbling stones, and the precision and earnest exactitude of the mouldings contrasts with the heavy Romanesque of the Tower. Yet it is a contrast within the same language and largely within the same technology; a twentieth-century architect could possibly produce an equally valid response, but both the language and the technology are irrevocably lost. A complex of social, technological, economic and aesthetic factors now exists which makes it impossible for the bridge ever to be reproduced, or to be repeated. These things also make its continued existence precarious.

The bridge takes its place in a great succession of structures connecting the two banks of London's river. Early inhabitants used the ford at Westminster, and the Romans used a ferry at the site of London Bridge. A timber bridge is mentioned as being in existence in 993, and in 1176 it was proposed, by a chaplain of the church in the Poultry in which Thomas à Beckett was baptised, that a

Left: the Pool of London, between Tower and London Bridges. At right, the Tower of London and St Katharine's Docks, now decayed and awaiting redevelopment

The Length of this Bridge is 237 Yd. the Heigh 15 Yards 1 Foot
And Stands upon 12 bold Arches but now there are only 9 in View
The rest being turned into Cellaring at the Building of the Key
To Cuthbert Fenwick Esq. the Right Worship.
Major of the Town of Newcastle upon Tine
This Plate is humbly dedicated by his most humble Servant John Kilburn
FORTITER TRIUMPHANS DEFENDIT
At the Entrance from the North Stands the Chapel of St. Thomas
Built about ye year 1200 This Bridge is of great Antiquity
Being in the time of the Romans Vid. Burns Page 127
J. Kilburn S.

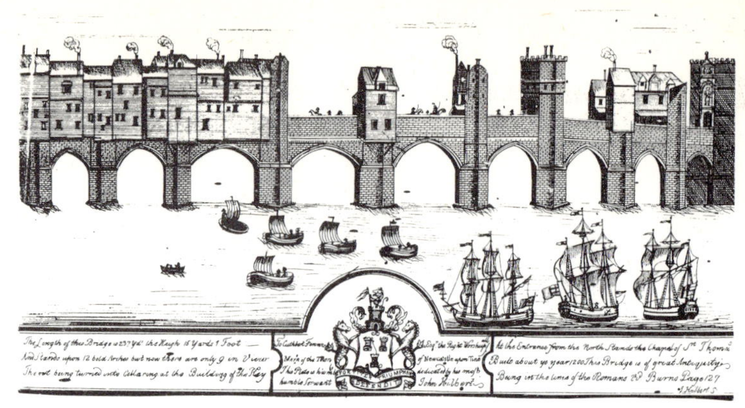

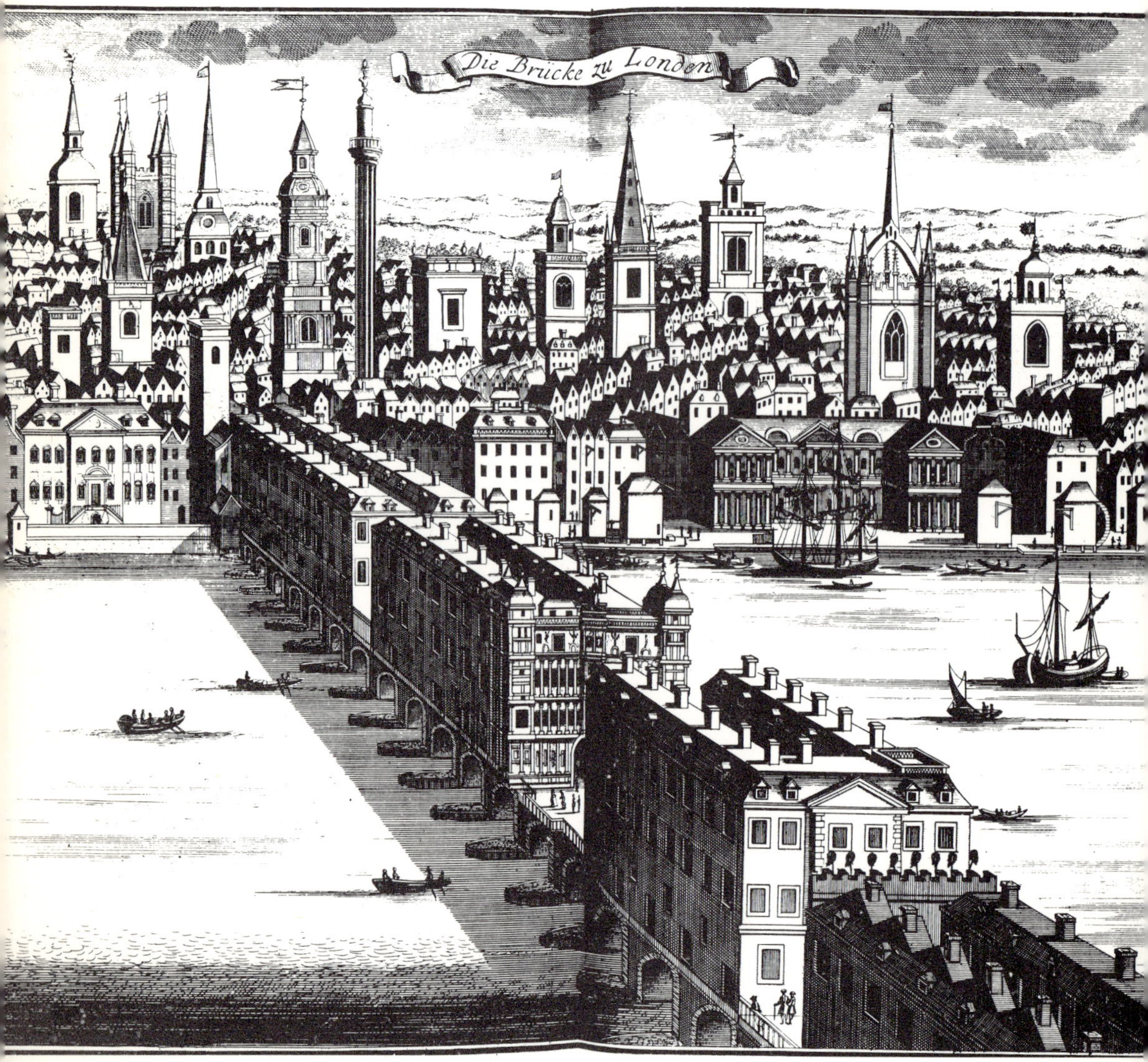

Die Brücke zu London

stone bridge should be built. This was completed by 1209, and the first London Bridge survived for 700 years. It was 926 feet long, 40 feet wide and near the middle, a span was opened by a drawbridge. The bridge was supported by nineteen arches, on piers 25-34 feet thick, carried on elm piles driven into the bed of the river. On the tenth pier was a chapel dedicated to St Thomas of Canterbury, and thus began the habit of building other structures integral with the bridge. (There were many other contemporary examples.) A tower was built on the north side in 1426, and houses from 1471. They were probably of timber, and burnt down in 1632 and 1666, but were always rapidly rebuilt.

Above left: the mediaeval bridge at Newcastle upon Tyne followed the pattern of old London Bridge
Left: London Bridge in 1735. Note the elegant and orderly structures resulting from the rebuilding of 1666, and the relation to the tower of St Magnus Martyr, whose porch marked the north end of the bridge

The funds for maintaining the bridge came from endowments of land, and from the revenue of the chapel. As these lands steadily increased in value over the centuries, their revenue has grown hugely. The Bridge House Estates have been able to rebuild London Bridge, build Blackfriars Bridge, and Tower Bridge, and to buy and allow free public use of Southwark Bridge. As Tower Bridge cost £902,500, excluding the cost of the land, a very considerable sum in 1895, the extent of the Bridge House Estates investments can be imagined.

Old London Bridge caused a tremendous blockage of the river. Its close-set piers, which were thickened from time to time with timber outworks to protect the piles on which it was built, formed a weir, so that the tide flow was considerably impeded. There was, even in an unexceptional tide, a difference of 5 feet between water level on either side of the bridge, making the passage under the bridge an exciting and dangerous undertaking. The flow of water was used in 1582, when water wheels were erected under the arches at the north end, to pump London's water supply. The stabilizing effect of the barrier on the upper reaches must have been considerable, making the use of the river much easier than it is now, and reducing the wear and scour on the banks.

The spans of old London Bridge varied from 10 to 30 feet and as ships grew bigger the need for a larger opening became apparent. An arch 70 feet wide was made in the centre of the span in 1759; some houses were cleared even earlier to make a proper carriage road. In the end the pressure of coach traffic became overwhelming. A new structure by Sir Charles Rennie was opened in 1831, at a cost of £1,500,000. This was well proportioned and beautiful, but a simple carriageway, and in its turn it was demolished in 1967 and transported to Lake Havasu City, Arizona, USA, one of the larger souvenirs. The newest bridge is an undistinguished motorway, though a separate pedestrian bridge is being provided at a higher level.

A monument in balance: Tower Bridge

It is an interesting comment that the iron bridges of the Thames, such as Tower Bridge, all turned out to be very much cheaper to build than the traditional stone bridges. They also retained their value to a greater extent when their private owners were bought out by the government in the late nineteenth century. London Bridge was sold for 2·46 million dollars (just under a million pounds in 1967).

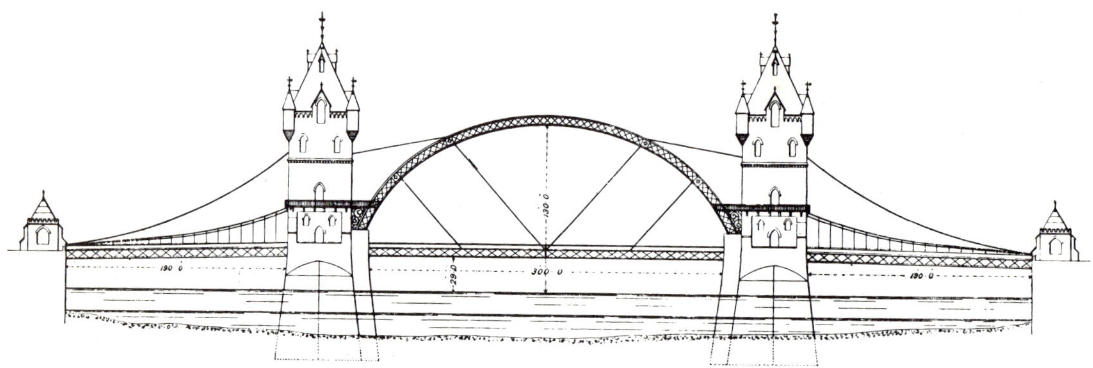

The vast growth of South and East London during the late nineteenth century produced an increasing demand for more bridges,* but the overriding requirements of the Board of the Thames Conservancy for free river access for ocean-going ships prevented any conventional solution east of London Bridge.

Sir Marc Isambard Brunel proposed a tunnel between Wapping and Rotherhithe in 1824, and after immense difficulties it was opened to pedestrians in 1843. The idea of vehicular traffic had to be abandoned because of the mounting expenses (£468,000) and the tunnel was afterwards sold to the East London Railway Company. Trains still use it.

The next move was the Tower Subway, an iron tube 7 feet in diameter from Great Tower Hill on the west side of the Tower to Pickle Herring Stairs on the south bank. This was opened in 1871 for pedestrians, and in spite of long access stairways nearly a million people used it each year, at a toll of ½d for each passage.

In May 1877 the City Architect, Sir Horace Jones, reported to his Bridge Committee on the alternative possibilities of the Tower Bridge site, and in the following year put forward the idea of the bascule bridge which after much argument was to find acceptance.

---

* A survey in August 1882 of London Bridge produced the daily user figures of 22,242 vehicles and 110,525 pedestrians, on a bridge only 54 feet wide.

A monument in balance: Tower Bridge

Above: Sir George Barclay Bruce's proposal of 1876 for a mechanical ferry
Left: Sir Horace Jones's first design for Tower Bridge in 1878, the basic idea for the final structure
Below: E. J. Palmer's proposal of 1877 for a double 'Duplex' bridge

In 1876 however Sir George Bruce had proposed a rolling bridge, a platform 300 feet × 100 feet which would move across a series of piers 100 feet apart. These would contain the rollers and driving machinery to propel this ingenious mechanical ferry from bank to bank.

An equally complex solution was the 'Duplex' Bridge, by F. J. Palmer, in 1877, which was a forerunner of another related proposal put up by a private company in 1884. Palmer's bridge consisted of two locks, with sliding spans to allow shipping to enter the lock; the span would then be closed, allowing vehicular traffic to move, while the alternative span slid away to allow the ship to move on. The complexity, and the small spaces available for the ships, made the idea unworkable.

A monument in balance: Tower Bridge

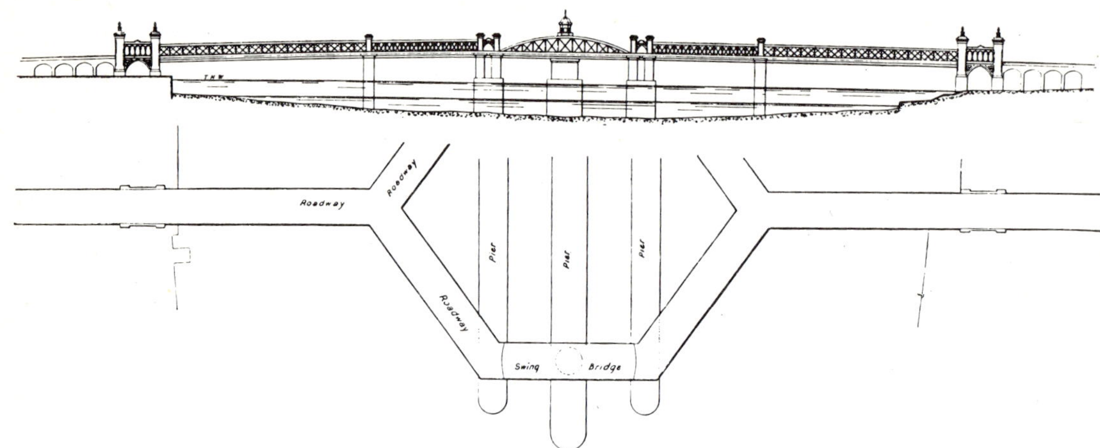

Above: the single 'Duplex' design by Bell and Miller, 1884
Below: the plan of Sir Joseph Bazalgette's proposals for a medium level bridge, showing the 5000 foot spiral southern approach gradient. The plan also shows the traditional method of mooring ships in tiers.

The revised proposal of 1884 had only a single lock, in the centre of the river, with double movable roadways at each end. Here again the width of the lock, and the cumbersome road approach, would have caused a great obstruction to river traffic.

The Metropolitan Board of Works applied to Parliament in 1879 to build a magnificent medium level bridge, designed by Sir Joseph Bazalgette, with an arched single span of 850 feet and a 65 feet clearance above high water. It would have been a wonderful structure, but involved great problems of access – particularly on the south side where a 5,700 feet long spiral ramp was proposed. (Sir Joseph had produced, on the same basic plan and approach system, two alternative designs, in 1878. They were for a cantilever, and for a lattice girder bridge.) The wharfingers, however, thought the clearance inadequate, and the idea was abandoned.

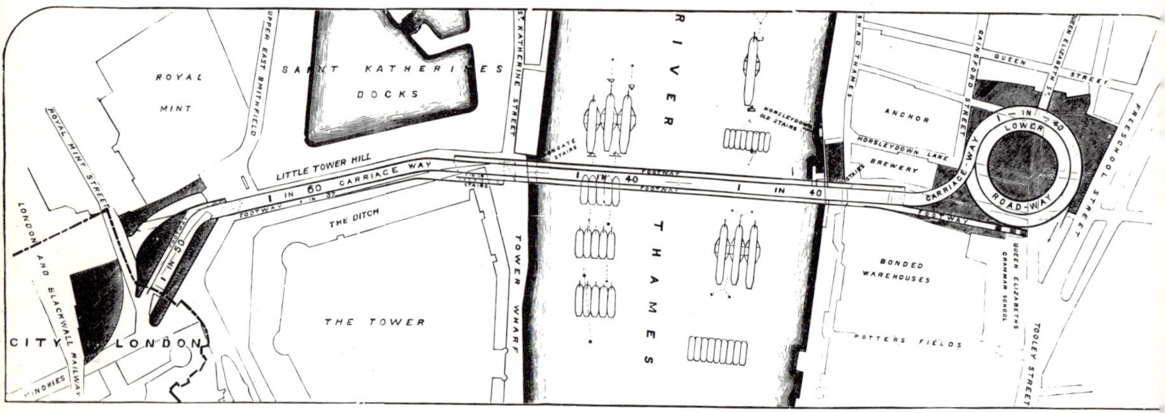

Above: Sir Joseph Bazalgette's famous design for a single span steel arch bridge which he produced in 1878
Below: alternative designs for cantilever and lattice girder bridges, with pier supports in the river, proposed by Sir Joseph in the same year. All three bridges would have used the same basic plan and approach level.

A monument in balance: Tower Bridge

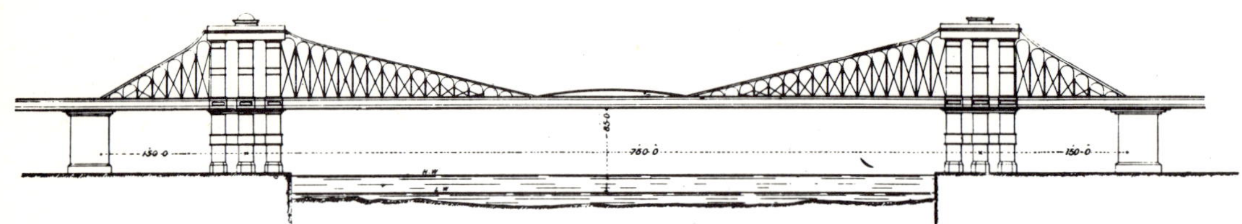

Above: an elegant medium level single span cantilever design by A. J. Sedley, 1879

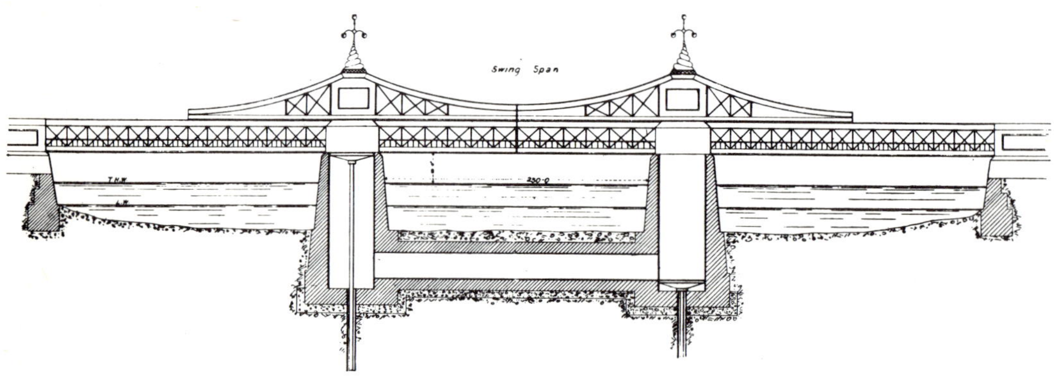

Above: the most logical design, a swing span by Knipple and Morris, 1884. Pedestrians would descend by lifts to a tunnel

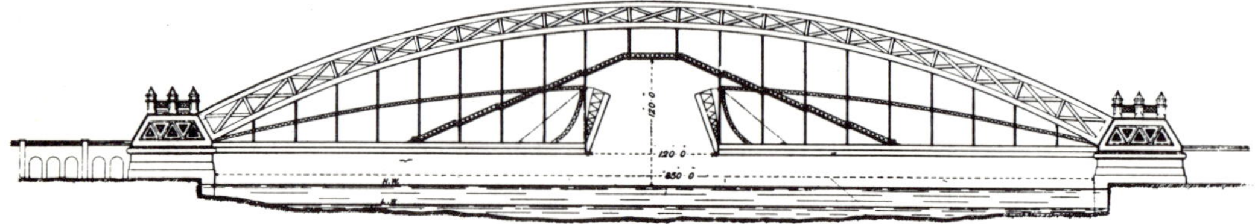

Above: a single-arched low level span, with bascules, by Ordish and Matheson, 1885

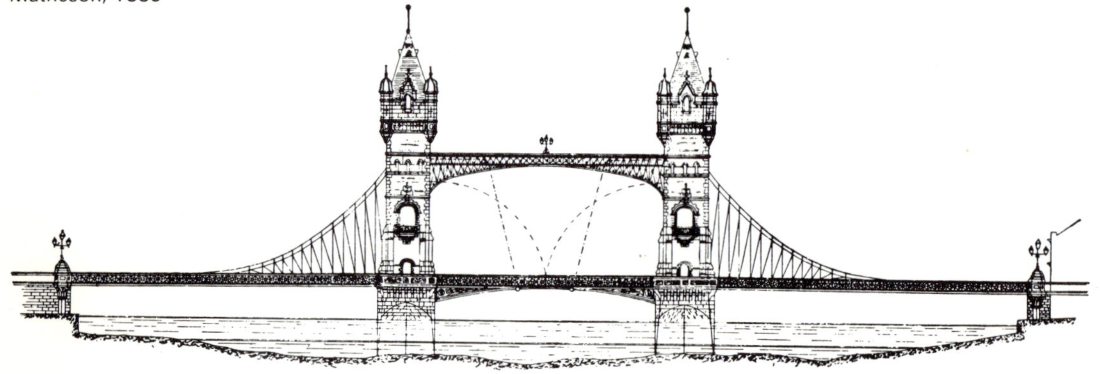

A monument in balance: Tower Bridge

In the 1883 Parliamentary session a private company proposed a tunnel, served by 'large and numerous hydraulic lifts', only to be opposed by the Metropolitan Board of Works, who produced their own plans for a tunnel the following year. This one had mile-long ramp approaches on both banks, and involved tremendous land acquisition costs.

The confusion caused by two very different proposals produced the usual parliamentary committee to examine the whole problem. After much consideration they decided that a low level bridge, with minimum problems of approach ramping, with an opening span, should be developed, and asked the City of London to undertake the work.

Yours faithfully
J Wolfe Barry

Above: portrait of Sir John Wolfe Barry
Left: the design by Jones and Barry approved by Parliament in 1885

This naturally brought the job to the Bridge House Estates Committee who, after appointing a deputation to visit the continent, Newcastle upon Tyne and other places with opening bridges, recommended Sir Horace Jones's original idea of 1878 for a bascule bridge.

His first proposal was for a steel arched structure over the main span, with main river piers very much as they are today, but in a rather French style. The difficulty was that the arched form did not allow the bascules to open completely, so that ships would be forced to stay precisely in the centre of the opening – which was a good deal to ask of sailing ships in a strong tide.

Sir Wolfe Barry was appointed as engineer for the bridge in 1884, and Sir Horace Jones as architect, and the impact of a fresh mind became at once apparent. The arch was dropped and a straight span substituted. The bascules could now open vertically, leaving the entire 200 feet span clear for shipping.

The revised design was approved by Parliament in 1885, and the long process of detail designing began.

The way in which the river was used at that time provided the basic layout. Vessels were moored in two, or sometimes three, parallel lines, head to stern, on either side of the river, leaving a clear 200-250 feet fairway down the middle. Goods were unloaded into barges for transport up river or to the bankside quays and warehouses.

Because the river use was relatively static some distance out from the banks, it was clear that the opening span need not be greater than the 200 feet wide fairway, with two side openings of some 300 feet which could be at a low level. Thus the position of the river piers was soon determined. In spite of the logic, the bridge

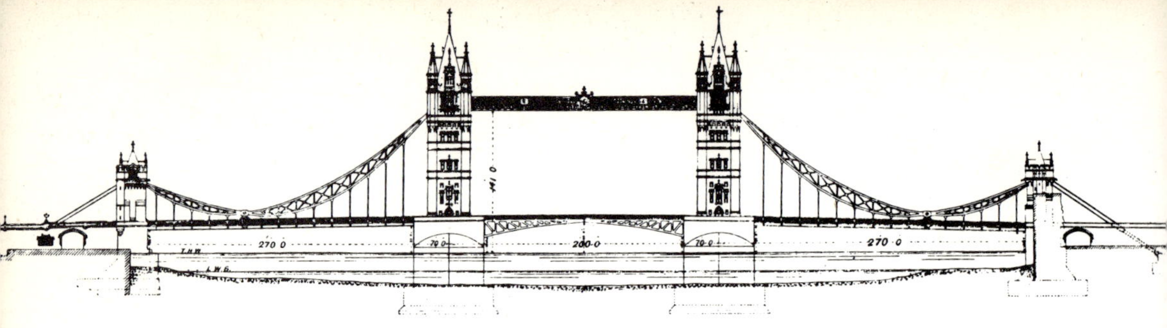

Above: the completed bridge by Sir John Wolfe Barry

Opposite and following pages: a selection of the architectural working drawings prepared by George D. Stevenson

was opposed by river users and the Conservancy and only passed through Parliament with several stringent conditions. The main requirements were that 160 feet of the central fairway should be kept open at all times (making it impossible to build more than one pier foundation at a time) and that the bridge be opened for two hours at high tide (which caused the elaborate provision of lifts and stairs for pedestrians to pass over at high level).

Because of the recent Tay Bridge disaster (1879), the Board of Trade required that all new structures be able to withstand wind pressures of 56 pounds per square foot; so that the mechanical provisions in the moving spans are somewhat excessive. The machinery required to work against this pressure was duplicated in each pier.

Parliament defined the opening span as 200 feet clear, 135 feet clearance above Trinity High Water when open and 29 feet when closed. The river piers were to be 185 feet long and 70 feet wide. Side spans were to be 270 feet clear.

Work began on 21st June 1886. The government allowed a small encroachment on the Tower Ditch, and in return required that the architecture of the bridge should accord with the Tower. Their other condition, that the bridge might be armed with guns, was afterwards abandoned, until an anti-aircraft battery was established on the river piers in 1940.

Sir Horace Jones intended a somewhat feudal architectural expression, in brick with stone dressings, and thought of the bridge working like a drawbridge in a castle, with chains. When Sir Wolfe came on the scene the engineering problems were critical and architectural considerations were put aside until the basic mechanisms were decided and the foundations were under way. Sir Horace died in 1887, before any architectural detail had been decided, and Sir Wolfe took control entirely. The programme had been much changed and, apart from the original concept, there is no doubt that the bridge owes its form and its mechanisms to Barry. It has an engineering straightforwardness that runs through all the details, and the precision and pedantry of the architecture is characteristic of the Victorian engineer. His architectural assistant, Mr Stevenson, was very much a part of a larger team of specialists.

TOWER BRIDGE

Elevation of East & West fronts Main Towers

0 10 20 30 40 50 60 70 80 90 100 feet

Scale of Feet

hames High Water Line

TOWER BRIDGE

Elevation of Main Towers facing Land Spans

0 5 10 20 30 40 50 60 70 80 90 100 feet

Scale of feet

High Water Line

533 116
TOWER BRIDGE
Detail of Top Stage East & West fronts of Main Towers
Scale of Feet
Portland Stone
Fine Axed Granite
Window dressings Portland Stone
Elevation
Rock faced Granite
Section on Centre Line

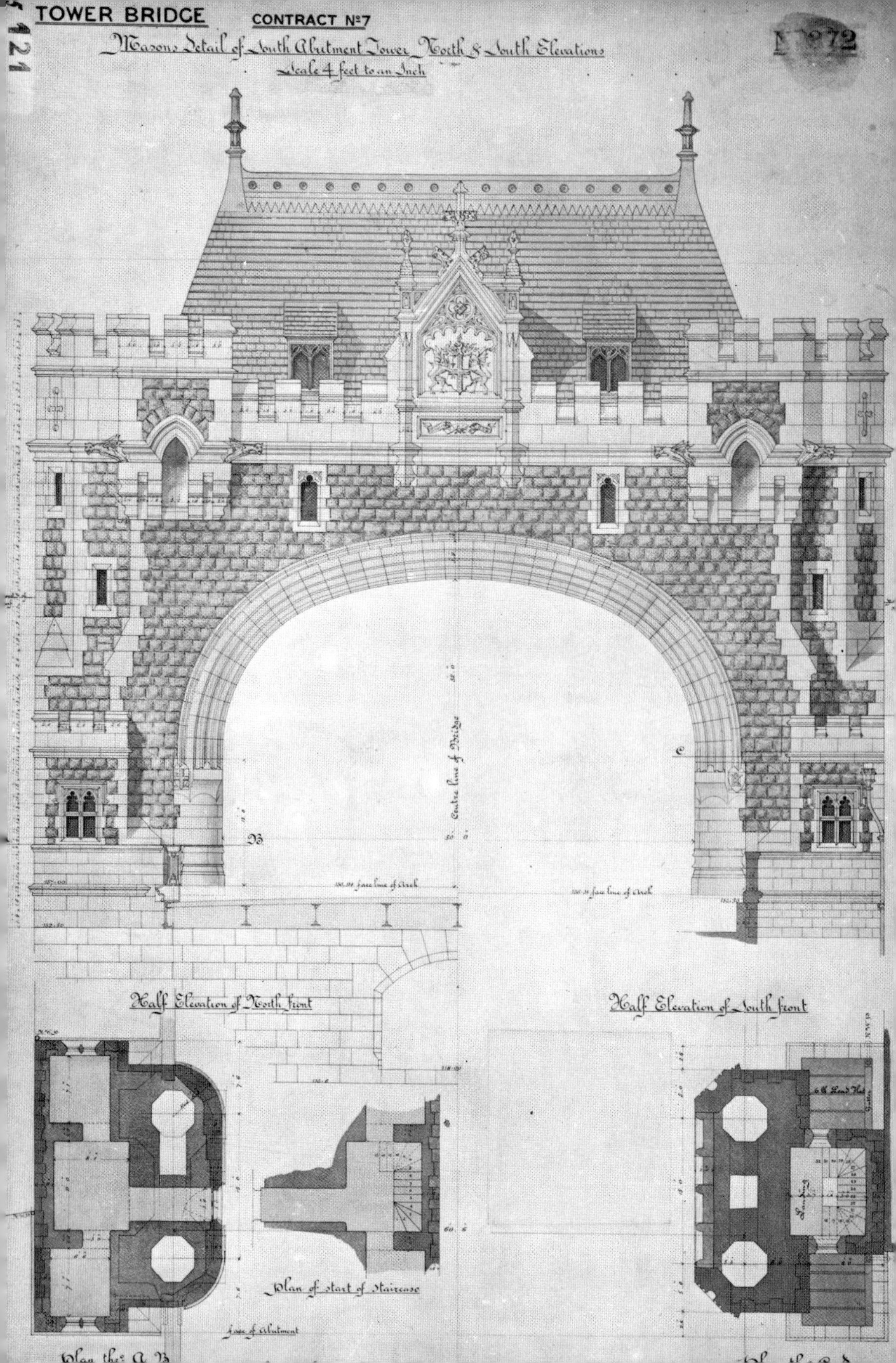
421
TOWER BRIDGE
CONTRACT Nº7
Nº 72
Masons Detail of South Abutment Tower North & South Elevations
Scale 4 feet to an Inch
Centre line of Bridge
face line of Arch
face line of Arch
Half Elevation of North front
Half Elevation of South front
Plan of start of Staircase
face of Abutment
Landing
6 lb Lead Flat

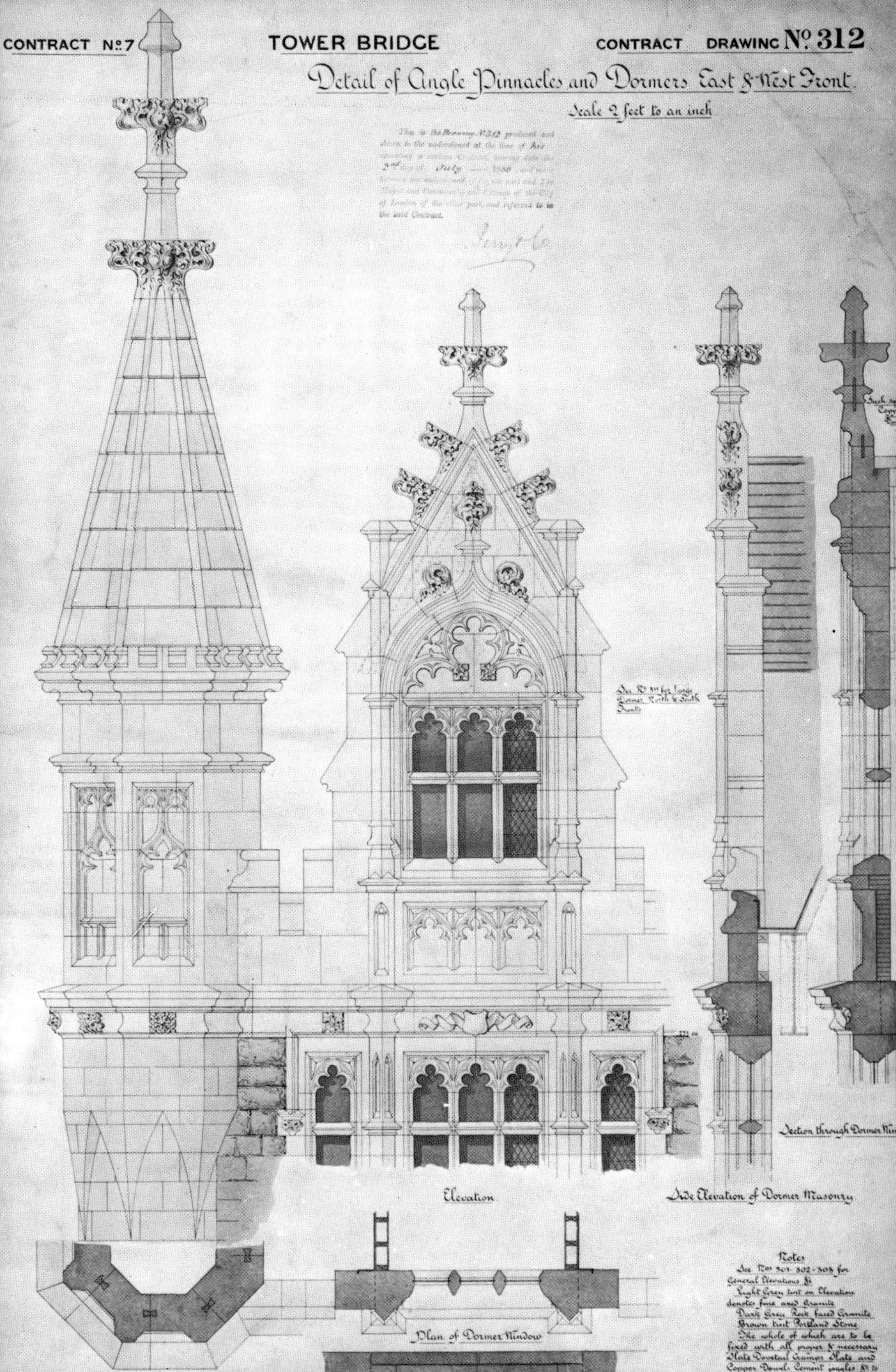
CONTRACT No. 7
TOWER BRIDGE
CONTRACT DRAWING No. 312
Detail of Angle Pinnacles and Dormers East & West Front.
Scale 2 feet to an inch
the said Contract.
Elevation
Side Elevation of Dormer Masonry
Plan of Dormer Window
Notes
See Nos 301-302-308 for
General Elevations &c
Light Grey tint on Elevation
denotes fine axed Granite
Dark Grey Rock faced Granite
Brown tint Portland Stone
The whole of which are to be
fixed with all proper & necessary
Slate Dovetail Cramps Slate and
Copper Dowels Cement joggles &c to

Tower Bridge today

Except at the south end, Tower Bridge shows few signs of wear or decay, though its surroundings are very much in process of change. On the north side, east of the Tower, is St Katharine's Docks, one of the great masterpieces of Victorian building, designed by Thomas Telford. These splendid warehouses, resting on Doric cast-iron columns, surround an enclosed pool, with lock gates to the river. They have been empty for many years and the future of the group has been in dispute. Because of their relatively small scale, the narrowness of the access lock and the now obsolete methods of handling cargo, they have shared the general decay of upriver docking. Andrew Renton's proposals for their intelligent redevelopment, with housing, offices and an entertainment complex, are very welcome. The basins become a yacht marina, and it is to be hoped that the artists, at present in one block, will remain.

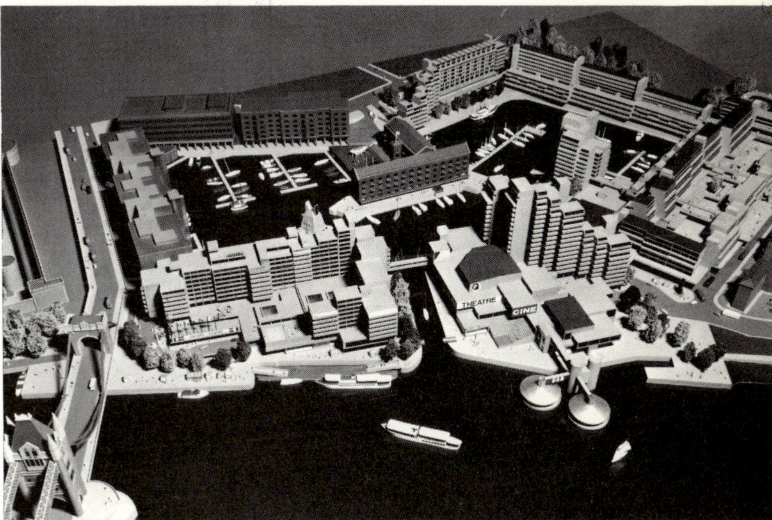

Above: the bridge from the Tower terrace
Above left: the west side with the brewery behind
Left: view from the east
Above right: the proposed redevelopment of St Katharine's Docks

The bridge itself is in remarkable condition; the original notices are still there, and the control cabins are well maintained, shiplike and tidy. The sensations on the bridge are marvellously complex, the web of steel against the sky, the vibration underfoot, the traffic on the roadway and, on the other side of the great thick balustrade, the river, boats and birds. The air of excitement and participation is a liberation of the spirit.

On the Tower side the riverside garden provides excellent views of the river and the bridge, and the small café there needs only to be lifted from its repulsive and obsolete squalor to become a very pleasant place.

The south side is rather more depressing. The long straight

approach, lined with nondescript buildings, is deflationary. On the west is a maze of bomb-damaged warehouses, which have not been replaced and whose function and value decrease yearly. The whole of this side of the Pool must very soon be rebuilt and the possibility of a mixed industrial, office, housing area with its own character is certainly there. The difficulty is that present planning methodology would almost certainly guarantee a desert of separated uses, and the high land cost makes any kind of more sophisticated intervention difficult. In areas such as this the difficulty of raising adequate capital forces a local authority to auction off its redevelopment rights (compulsory purchase powers) to the highest commercial bidder. In turn the developer, to safeguard his own position, will provide only those elements (offices, factory space) which produce the highest immediate return. This elementary sequence automatically produces a complex entirely lacking in complexity, without those marginal uses which give nuance, quality and life to an environment. Perhaps we should hopefully wait until the shipping use has resolved itself into a new pattern before making plans, and who knows, by then we may know how to state the problem of redevelopment correctly.

Above: the memorial stone on the north side
Above right: the bridge seen from the Tower
Right: the north approach

The southeast side of the bridge is dominated by the large Courage Brewery which, like most breweries, is a maze of alterations and additions that give a pleasantly romantic skyline.

At this side, too, is the main accumulator house (see page 117), a simple cube of brickwork – a little drab perhaps – but intended to be read as part of the street rather than of the bridge. Beside it is a stair down to the roadway under the Surrey approach, which leads to the boilers and engine room. Here the maintenance is somewhat less respectful. This working area shares the squalor we have come to think of as inherent in work, and has its origin perhaps in the handling of coal. An elaborate system of hydraulic cranes was provided to lift coal from barges to small railway trucks, which then ran to the coal store in an arch between the engines and the boilers. When the floor was filled with coal, the trucks were raised by an hydraulic lift to an overhead conveyor running the length of the store, tipping on either side. As coal is now delivered by road the mess is somewhat greater and the servicing more haphazard. The boundary to the west is poorly defined by a bombed warehouse.

The upper works of the towers are little used. The river piers are empty halls over the roadway, and the shore piers contain, on the north side, flats for the staff, and on the south side the administration offices.

The vibration of the traffic makes the use of the accommodation difficult, and the staff prefer to live away from the job.

Above: detail of the north shore tower
Right: The north shore tower seen through the arch of the river pier

Above: the north suspension span with Telford's St Katharine's Docks beyond
Right: detail of a window in the river tower

Tower Bridge today

Above: the north west control cabin
Right: detail of the suspension chain
Far right: connection of suspension span to the balustrade
Below: signal at the control cabin

ONTINEN
WHARVES

Above: detail of the City Coat of Arms over the shore towers
Right: a detail of the river tower

Above: the pinnacles on the river towers with the high level bridge
Right: a niche and window in the south river tower

Junctions of steel and stone
Above: the housing of the suspension span into the shore towers
Right: the tie from the Surrey bank to the shore tower
Far right: the suspension span housed into the river tower

A page of details
Above: a finial over a river tower niche
Right: a lintel on the river tower
Above right: carving at the base of a niche

Above: notice at the control cabin
Right: sign at the north tower arch

Above: view from the bridge south-east to the picturesque Courage Brewery
Far right: a detail of the massive connection to the suspension span
Right: gantry at the control cabin, with fine cast iron railings

The social connection

The social connection

Perhaps the most valuable of Tower Bridge's functions is one which it fulfills badly, but which it inherits, as no other Thames crossing, from Old London Bridge. Tower Bridge is still a place to walk on; it invites a crossing by its promise of a complex architectural experience, its promise of something shared: a marvellous series of views up and down stream, a participation in the working life of the river (as opposed to the working life of the streets which other bridges convey), and an involvement in the drama of the Pool. The latter is a complex socio-historic phenomenon: big ships, cranes, Customs House, Tower, St Magnus Martyr, Billingsgate, the tottering warehouses. The sensations of participating in history, in the activity of the Fish Market, in the work and life of the ships and seamen are deliciously interwoven. This multitude of experiences, intricately and subconsciously overlaid, is the very stuff of cities, the product of a rich mix of uses and associations, and itself the justification of the romantic view of cities. It is the rewarding end product of complexity (and it has also a very real cash value).

It is this quality of participation that Tower Bridge has inherited from Old London Bridge. The latter was at once a barrier to shipping (it marked the limit for ocean-going ships) and a barrage for the tide. The effect was to slow down tidal change above the bridge and produce a higher and more stable water level, which in turn helped the users of the river and ensured an equalizing growth on both banks. The river was not a barrier in the way it became in the nineteenth century and remains today, though there was only one bridge for 700 years. In fact, the provision of other bridges was strenuously resisted by the City of London merchants.

Old London Bridge was primarily a shopping street. This extra use provided a permanent and highly sophisticated value link between the two banks. Above the shops were houses, including many famous and beautiful buildings, so that the continuity of the city was virtually uninterrupted from side to side.

All this has gone, to be replaced only by a series of windy carriageways. The lack of this lifeline, this vital link, is probably the main cause of the catastrophic decline of the south bank in the nineteenth century. And it is certain that nothing will regrow that depressed area until some similar connection is made to the north shore. The creation of a series of cultural monoliths, isolated in a few acres of concrete, will solve nothing, and produce nothing except a demand for more subsidies.

It is the intervention of commercial life, of individual initiatives in creating the small elements of identity that establishes a living city.

The social connection

Above: one of the control cabins, of which there are four, one on each side of the river piers

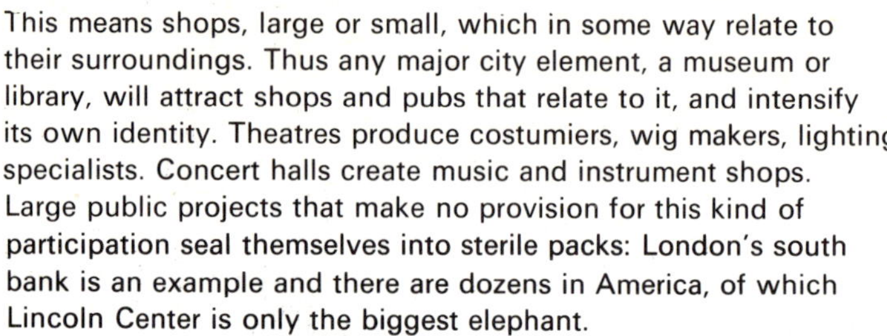

This means shops, large or small, which in some way relate to their surroundings. Thus any major city element, a museum or library, will attract shops and pubs that relate to it, and intensify its own identity. Theatres produce costumiers, wig makers, lighting specialists. Concert halls create music and instrument shops. Large public projects that make no provision for this kind of participation seal themselves into sterile packs: London's south bank is an example and there are dozens in America, of which Lincoln Center is only the biggest elephant.

Old London Bridge, which died in 1824 to be replaced by Rennie's beautiful but elementary structure, could also be considered as a prototypical route-building, a connector element in the city and a major encloser of space. Its position as first bridge would have made the space open ended downstream, so that the strong sense of enclosure experienced today was lacking. On the other hand, the river was more used, a maze of vessels and rigging. Its relation to the Church of St Magnus Martyr, whose porch was on the east pavement of the bridge and whose tower signalled the city, was singularly beautiful and poetic.

The realignment of the bridge approach at a higher level further upstream has destroyed the church, wedged behind a marine warehouse and office block, and this must be counted a major loss. But it is still there, a grace note, and an element of history and poignancy in the scene.

The bridge carried a great variety of houses, with shops underneath. Although they were several times burnt, the shops were quickly rebuilt; and they were probably much altered and adapted as time went on. Many were famous examples of the architecture of the period, including Nonsuch House.

Though Tower Bridge has something of this quality of an artery, of a connection, it has nothing with which to connect. The south bank is exceptionally barren just here. It would make an exceedingly interesting experiment to attempt to grow something at the south abutment, to match the Tower and its garden café on the other side.

The extraordinary machinery of the bridge, the great pumps and accumulators, could be a real attraction. The area could be cleaned up and made visible to spectators. The vast brewery on the east side might be persuaded to provide a pub, a balcony and a pier for river craft.

Minimal expenditure perhaps, but a link in a chain of social and economic value.

Above and below lett: one of the great engines in the boiler room under the south approach. The beautiful and well maintained machines, brightly painted, are some of the few remaining examples of Victorian mechanical engineering, and should be one of the sights of London

In making this kind of gesture to the south bank the possibility of a civilized redevelopment of that depressed area becomes closer. The long term profitability of an area depends, ultimately, on its social dynamic and self-regenerative capacity. To rebuild everything every twenty years places a tremendous strain on capital formation. Our tendency towards larger and larger units, in business and in building, makes us forget that the economic problems of replacement, as well as of maintenance, are not eased by increase of scale. When an individual or a small organization might make an impact on a city, with a single building, or even by a redecoration, the burden and benefit of urban growth can be widely spread. Thus a small scale area with many varied owners and users will always by its cycle of random cleaning, painting and alteration demonstrate its inner dynamic, and because of the multiplicity of parts it is less liable to a general blight.
Individual operators are seldom all equally affected by single economic factors. Large organizations, on the other hand, which follow the monopolizing trend in our technology, are singularly unprepared for adverse economic trends. They retreat and retrench. It is just this scale of big business, national rather than local, which is inevitably irresponsible at the environmental level. It could hardly be otherwise. The directors of national or international

companies are too concerned with the macro-scale to think of the effect on local values their operations may have. They are not concerned with places, but with balance sheets that plot the profitability of their properties. That is, their concern with building is simplistic, purely economic. When a company is swallowed by a large corporation its local ties and responsibilities are cut, its buildings suddenly become unreal. They are no longer the responsibility of a proud founder, but of an administrator concerned with standardization and economy. In any case the current mode of thinking about environmental problems by big corporations – prestige headquarters controlling a scattered empire of sordid back-street factories – makes their involvement dangerous.

Sensitive areas in cities (and nearly all areas in cities are sensitive because people live in them), are therefore best removed from the world of the big company.* Cities are seedbeds, and they grow enterprises. In the early stages of company growth, the firm needs local support and services. With success it can move outwards to larger, more logically arranged premises. But to attempt to pre-empt the seedbed itself for its mature life is a sure way of reducing future growth, and enterprise, in the neighbourhood.

Thus the planning agency is confronted with a dichotomy. On one side the corporations can raise capital and be trusted with large areas of redevelopment, though the end result is guaranteed sterile.†

---

* Corporations: the big grow much bigger.
'The very largest companies are taking over a steadily growing share of US business. Fortune's annual listing of the top 500, published last week, shows that the biggest industrial companies rang up almost 64% of all industrial sales in the US last year, up from 62% in 1967 and just over 55% a decade ago. In their fields the 500 employed 687 out of every 1,000 workers and accounted for 74% of total profits. Despite the tax surcharge, profits were up 13%, to $24 billion.
General Motors again led the list, followed in the top ten by Standard Oil (NJ), Ford, General Electric, Chrysler, IBM, Mobil Oil, Texaco, Gulf Oil and US Steel. Collectively, the top ten increased earnings by 21%, or double the rate of the other 490 companies.
The trend of the 500 underscores the growing importance of "economies of scale." Size clearly offers the opportunity for more efficient use of equipment and greater market clout.' *Time* May 1969.

† Of the many examples we might quote the Shell Centre in London or the Central Electricity Generating Board complex round St Paul's. An instructive early example is the replacement of the Adams Brothers' Adelphi by Shell-Mex House in the 'thirties, a blow from which the area has not yet recovered.
Almost every US city has been devastated on a much larger scale, in a similar way: the Golden Triangle in Pittsburgh is a vast area of new office blocks without even a decent restaurant; the St Louis downtown waterfront replaced acres of cast iron warehouses with banal glass towers still half empty (no restaurant there either). In Paris, the Gare Montparnasse redevelopment is only a forerunner of what is promised for the Halles in the centre of the city.
For a critique of the new city see *Playtime*, a film by Jacques Tati.

On the other there is a tremendous financial gamble if smaller firms are involved. The compromise is inevitably to involve the developer who, backed by the insurance companies, tries to hedge his bet with standard shopfronts suitable only for supermarkets and chain stores, and standard office blocks which he will hope to rent to the government or a corporation.

Perhaps there is no way out of this impossible choice except to reduce the scale of operations to one dictated by actual need, rather than attempting to create a need which may not be there at all. Property development is a gamble, which depends largely on inflation to bring a profit. All economic factors including population and productivity increases would seem to push for higher and higher property values, but in practice it is very difficult to create an area from scratch. Great subtlety in the matter of rents and incentives is required to get tenants, and it may be that more involvement, on the smaller scale, will bring about the stability so necessary in development. Thus a tenant with a stake in the whole, or a complete control over a part, has an involvement which no other form of participation can bring. He brings his life, his heart and mind to his environment.

There is no denying that a process of piecemeal growth, and complex involvement of many people on different conditions, is both difficult, uncertain, and for the developer, unprofitable and tiresome. To be at all possible it requires a small scale of operation, and the renunciation of the great speculative profits of recent years. But the alternatives are more dangerous.

The process of city growth requires participation, and reactions. To begin a chain reaction it is necessary to provide a gesture or trigger from which other decisions can be made. To make the decisions all at once (as in a housing estate) is to anticipate or abort all reaction from the participants: their contribution is thereafter largely negative and often destructive. But the introduction of something other, an element which is random or illogical, may be a good beginning. It is this function which is filled by the monument; and Tower Bridge is an excellent example of a trigger mechanism.

The future of monuments

The future of monuments

It is perfectly possible to calculate the capacity of a road with a fair degree of accuracy and it has become obvious that Tower Bridge has reached its limits as a road. It is often jammed. The volume of traffic must, according to all the statistics, regularly increase for many years to come, doubling by 1980.

At the same time, technology makes changes in the bridge's other functions: shipping grows less and less in the Pool: St Katharine's Docks are deserted and the owners of the remaining warehouses would dearly love to replace them with offices.

The tendency in shipping is towards containers, standard units of cargo which can be mechanically handled and stacked. For efficiency, the process requires a large unobstructed area, in order to marshal trucks and trains, for the conveyors and transporters. Such areas are available at Tilbury and Gravesend, with good and improving road and rail access. The London Docks are obsolete and archaic, and their continued existence is due entirely to habit and inertia.

Though no official consideration has been given to the future of the bridge – a highly emotive subject – it is clear that some thought is required. To replace it with a tunnel would solve both the road and river problems in a very characteristically twentieth-century way, by removing both the pain and the pleasure from the situation. It would carry many more vehicles and would not be subject to delays caused by shipping. It would be reasonably economical, but the bridge, its emotive impact and its intangible value, would be lost. Another, more sophisticated, proposal is to build a relief road, or roads, in tunnels further downstream. Traffic is cramped on both sides down river, the banks are lined with decaying warehouses and factories, and many possible connections could be made, which would draw the pressure from the bridge. With sufficient alternative routes a traffic balance may be achieved within its environmental capacity.

Such a policy would maintain one section of the status quo, but would not affect the shipping. It is possible that the gradual disappearance of ocean-going shipping from the Pool will automatically retire the ageing engines of the bridge, and thus neatly solve the problem. It would also be possible to hasten the process by Act of Parliament, closing the Pool, and compensating its present users. The bridge would be left firmly down, and we would once again simplify the problem, and lose a spectacle, the bascules in action.

Left: Tower Bridge is perhaps the only bridge in the world constantly visited by summer tourists

A further alternative would be to depend entirely on relief tunnels for motor traffic, and leave the bridge permanently open only to shipping. This puts us neatly into the worst possible situation, reducing the pedestrian use of the bridge to nothing and destroying an adequate, though limited capacity, cross river route, for the sake of a dwindling shipping use.

The logic, therefore, seems to be to hold on to the present structure as long as any basic elements of its use continue, allowing it to function in its original way for as long as possible. Adjustment of road and shipping traffic may be required to keep its environmental balance, but they are slight penalties compared to the massive urban and emotional benefits.

Because Tower Bridge is still in operation, its gradual decline in the face of changing functions can be easily observed. This decline has already been completed in the case of many equally important nineteenth-century monuments. London's Euston Arch and New York's Penn Station have gone; in New York Grand Central Station, and in London St Pancras Railway Station and Gilbert Scott's Foreign Office are still under fire. At the scale of these great buildings, many created and still owned by private enterprise, the individual is helpless. These dinosaurs are too big and too expensive to be dealt with except at government level. Here our literary minded bureaucracy finds itself with a problem for which it is not equipped. There is no tradition of spending money to rescue buildings, and, above all, no imaginative enterprise in infusing such buildings with new life, and new uses.

Well-made buildings, even if they have long since repaid their original capital, are seldom incapable of restoration and renewal. Properly funded and maintained, they are self-regenerating economic organisms, as vast areas of seventeenth-and eighteenth-century London and Paris convincingly prove. The Temple, Belgravia, Regent's Park, the Ile St Louis and vast stretches on both sides of the Seine retain their values, repair themselves, are actually enriched by passing time.

Threatened buildings, such as St Pancras Station, require to be reassessed, and revalued at every level*; alternative uses can be suggested which provide the basis for a new existence, which can then be made a reality only by imaginative financial policies.
In the case of Tower Bridge, the value of the structure as urban decoration is overwhelming, and now far outranks its original traffic functions. It must be the only bridge in the world constantly

---

* St Pancras Station, for example, might make a very adequate exhibition hall, the vast cellars serving as workshops, the hotel public rooms being used for conferences, the bedrooms refurbished, or used as administrative offices.

Above: the south bank of the Pool of London, an area becoming daily more obsolete. The regeneration of this dismal stretch without the declining shipping use will depend on its pedestrian connection to the prosperous north side
Below: the terrace of the Tower

filled with summer visitors, marvelling, and enjoying the views and the place. In a leisure society, this is a tangible and rapidly growing asset.

The Tower of London is one of the world's greatest tourist attractions; apart from the building's romantic history, it houses the Crown Jewels, an unsurpassed collection of armour, and a Romanesque chapel. Much of this value spills over to the bridge and it is very noticeable how many people walk across it, only to be shocked and bored by the inhospitable south bank. Interest tapers off rapidly and the tourist beats a hasty retreat.

It is policy to revitalize the south bank and many ponderous projects are under way further up river. Plans have been put forward for a riverside walk, partly floating, and there is a steady growth in awareness of London's river, as it changes from a commercial to a possible leisure and tourist asset. The great rise in boat ownership, the many proposals for marinas and other facilities, and such great projects as the Thames barrage, will tend to recreate the busy river scene of the eighteenth century. Under the south approach road are the bridge's great engines, original and perfect, a possible nucleus for a leisure enterprise.

The future of monuments

The future of monuments

Above and left: tourists at Tower Bridge, the ever renewed raw material of our greatest future industry

Cities live by enterprise. In the late twentieth century, and in the next, we can be sure that Britain's role is unlikely to be an imperial one; the British will have to live on their wits. Britain already attracts a vast tourist trade, which can only grow. If a reasonable decency is to be maintained in tourist areas, it must be accepted that they too have an environmental capacity.

In short, it is necessary to create, or discover, new monuments to spread the load, to even out the pressures on Westminster Abbey and the Tower. These necessary treasures stand, ignored, all round us in the great heritage of Victorian and Edwardian buildings. The theoretical evaluation and appreciation of these buildings is now well under way, and the government has recently taken great steps to encourage preservation, and to prevent the careless greed that destroys one listed building of architectural importance *every* day.

Unfortunately, Ministerial admonitions are inevitably a little late, and are generally negative; a preservation order forbidding change.

Britain has a system which lists over 100,000 buildings as of historical importance, but relatively weak controls. Some countries have very powerful controls, but, as in France, over a mere 15,000 buildings. Others have hardly any. In the US even the award of a 'landmark' plaque is no safeguard against demolition by an owner who feels that the ultimate dollar may be escaping him.

It is therefore necessary, and urgent, that a more positive attitude towards our herd of white elephants is adopted. We must begin to see them for what they are: ASSETS. Assets in cities to stand against the serried curtain walls; assets which remind us of the continuity and meaning of city life; assets which provide an escape and a relief from the overwhelming coherence, the one-dimensionality, of our culture.

Assets, however, such as these depend on our attitude towards them. In the dark ages the Romans forgot their history; temples and arches disappeared. With their rediscovery and restoration they more than earn their keep today. Our new monuments need to be similarly discovered, to be publicized, and, above all, they must be allowed to survive until their value is accepted.

Death of a monument: Pennsylvania Station

Death of a monument: Pennsylvania Station

Above: the statue of Cornelius Vanderbilt, founder of the New York Central Lines, at the foot of the south front of Grand Central Station
Left: Park Avenue with the north side of Pan Am building entirely dominating the original tower. McKim, Mead & White's Racquet Club building at right indicates the original scale of this explosively changed street

In the nineteenth century the railways carried the same emotional charge as does the aircraft in our own time. Everything happily yielded to this new technology, which with all its convenience, speed and safety, still inflicted terrible wounds on town and country. These wounds remain unhealed. The urge to bring the steam train into the heart of the city was universal, and nowhere more ruthless and ingenious than in New York. As in European cities, the railway stations were conceived as triumphal termini, the seal or crown of the transportation achievement. This pride produced, until quite recently, some of the greatest expenditure (and thus the most valuable and meaningful monuments) of our cultural history. Nineteenth-century architects brought to their work an immense industry, and a hard-won respect for the language of previous architecture. It was an age of measuring. Their sketchbooks were full of useful details from their cultural travels, which were worked up into immensely complex structures. Their confidence and their competence were immense, and from the great engineers they learned that all problems could be solved by industry and application.

The two great termini in New York are Grand Central, and the Pennsylvania station. Each is an example of the collapse of a great building in the face of change. Grand Central is one of the engineering wonders of the world: layers of railway tracks under Park Avenue terminating in splendid Roman halls. The great tower which marked the station effectively dominated the miles long stretch of Park Avenue and the stately hotels and apartments on either side.

After World War II the area, always fashionable, became a target for developers eager to turn the value of the street to their own ends. The first new building, Lever House, was also the first of the glass skyscrapers. It set a style that has conquered the world, a glass box on a two storey podium. Its relation to the neighbouring stone-faced cliffs was both churlish and inefficient, but the image of the glass tower, which had haunted modern architecture since the 'twenties, had become a reality.

Soon after, an infinitely more serious building was built diagonally across the street. Mies van der Rohe and Philip Johnson's Seagram Building fitted precisely the four storey blocks at its rear and made a memorable group with the brownstones at the side and McKim, Mead & White's Racquet Club opposite. For a few years a remarkable urban sensation existed, ordered serenity. However, it was not long before the pressure on the adjoining buildings grew intense and they and the whole street rapidly turned into a forest of glass blocks, indifferently reflecting each other. The Pan Am building, the largest work by Walter Gropius,

Death of a monument: Pennsylvania Station

Above: detail and left, general view of the south side of Grand Central Station

loomed over the Grand Central building and suddenly it wasn't there any more. And neither was Seagram. It was swallowed up in the maze.

The technical problems of threading the foundations of a building as large as Pan Am through four layers of railways tracks were immense; their triumphant resolution is an enormous feat of US technology. At the end of it all the building, though gigantic in scale and entirely humourless, is somehow a success, probably because the top is a landing pad for the airport helicopter service (a splendid example of multiple use). In place of the spires of the early skyscrapers (each was often an extraordinary architectural invention) the sight of the mechanical butterflies rising from the Pan Am building gives an equivalent sense of excitement and of participation in the twentieth century.

From the south side of Park Avenue, Pan Am is set well back behind the station entrance, and its sunlit façade always looks good. Pressure for air space is, however, so intense that another similar block was proposed to be built over the great waiting halls on the south side. Here the low building is at present dominated only by a splendid and elaborate sculptural group which symbolizes the railway terminal, and gives notice of the spectacular Roman interior. The vast halls in the rush hour (a truly terrifying spectacle) by their height and grandeur make bearable the intense press of humanity. The effect of physical pressure and tension which in the new Penn station turns one almost immediately to neurosis and hysteria, is here somehow released. The psychological effect of 'waste' space is nowhere more clearly demonstrated. These halls (and those of the old Penn station) are necessary healing elements in the competitive city.

The passing of Grand Central station* as a nineteenth-century monument is a loss, but at least it has been overlaid by buildings of an even wilder improbability and monumentality, and the net result is probably a gain.

---

* 'French in spirit, but with no evident prototypes, is the Grand Central station, New York, built in 1903-13 by Reed & Stem and Warren & Wetmore. More efficiently organized than the Pennsylvania Station, its concourse is one of the grandest spaces the early twentieth century ever enclosed'. Thus Henry-Russell Hitchcock in *Architecture nineteenth and twentieth centuries* Penguin Books 1958.
He notes that the 'organization of the tremendous complex was probably the work of Charles A. Reed (?-1911) and Allan H. Stem (1856-1931)', veteran railway architects. Whitney Warren (1864-1943) and Charles D. Wetmore (1866-1941) were probably responsible for the 'dignified and well scaled detailing'.

MADISON SQUARE GARDEN CENTER
CANTEEN

PENNSYLVANIA STATION

Death of a monument: Pennsylvania Station

Such is not the case of Pennsylvania station where a technically competent but architecturally callow structure has replaced McKim,

reduced to a bare minimum, with low, mean spaces and corridors to accommodate an awesome number of people. Above the squalor rises the usual office block and the new Madison Square Garden sports arena.

The ingredients of a wonderful building existed in the programme, a truly complex brief in both the technical and developmental sense. Yet nobody has risen to the occasion. By separating the arena from the office block the architects have simplified their problems. They have also reduced the meaning of the total complex. An age confident of its architectural language would have attempted an integration. It is precisely this failure, and the hundreds like it, that throw the whole problem of city redevelopment into question, and which reinforce the negative, protectionist argument. Hardly anyone wishes to preserve anything without good reason, but one can be almost certain under present conditions that a new building will be a bad building. The gradually stiffening controls over building all over the world are a part of a growing public reaction to the poor quality of modern commercial architecture.

Left: the new Pennsylvania Station, an entirely undistinguished office block
Below left: the main entrance, used by many thousands daily
Below: the office block with the new Madison Square Gardens arena at right

Death of a monument: Pennsylvania Station

Above left: McKim, Mead & White's design for Pennsylvania Station
Above: the general waiting room
Left: the restaurant
Following page: the concourse of the now demolished station

The partnership of McKim, Mead & White was the dominant force in American architecture from 1880 to world war I. Both McKim and White had been pupils of H. H. Richardson but they moved away from his ponderous Romanesque style to something more in keeping with the time, a period of remarkable wealth and growing sophistication. Their buildings are not extraordinary when one comes across them, just very good in a matrix of building which is often of incredibly high standard. Their great contribution is that they profoundly influenced their contemporaries into a sober, Roman style, an achievement (according to Sir Charles Reilly) to compare with the effect of Wren or Jones. Charles Follen McKim was born in 1847, Stanford White in 1853. W. R. Mead, the business partner, joined in 1880 and the firm grew vastly over the years to become the prototypical plan-factory (such as Skidmore, Owings and Merrill in our own time) that was essential for construction on the American scale. Their buildings, once the great operation was established, became inevitably more mechanical, particularly after the death of the original designer partners, McKim in 1909 and White in 1906. The decline is said to date from the death of Joseph M. Wells, an associate of the firm, in 1891, whose Villard houses had set the firm on its academic career.

Their incredibly numerous works include the University Club, the library at Columbia University, the Tiffany Building, Madison Square Church, Madison Square Gardens, National City Bank, the Morgan Library, Penn Station, all in New York.

Death of a monument: Pennsylvania Station

Death of a monument: Pennsylvania Station

Above: the only available view of Pennsylvania station. There is an extraordinary lack of documentation on this enormous and important building

For centuries, central areas of cities have been the mainsprings of intellectual and social life. In prototypical US cities central areas are today run down and deserted, or else well advanced on the cycle of slum, followed by clearance, followed by commercial redevelopment or the new permanent slum of the low cost housing project. Within these miserable, minimum blocks there is no hope of growth, assimilation or change; no prospect but violence and alienation.

In this cycle the middle classes leave the city and do not return.

The source of city decay is richly complex. Its roots are in the very heart of our modes of perception, in the methods we have of measuring ourselves and in our idea of progress. In the worship of growth and productivity we have been unable to conceive ends, only means. We need more and more of everything, endlessly, and our industrial base and our living standards depend on it. The static, slowly evolving city of the past cannot stretch to accommodate the new dream of rapid and continuous expansion.

In the world of the developer, always piratical, the search for a higher productivity has brought an intense scrutiny into every aspect of building and in the process the architect has been largely eliminated. In central areas, buildings are readily calculated by estate agents' clerks and their values and specifications are pretty much the application of routine standards. Frills are never contemplated, thus unnecessary to eliminate. After all is settled, the architect is appointed to apply the module of his choice.

The concentration on ever higher returns, on stringent economies in all directions, results, without exception, in poor architecture. History is full of examples of mean streets and meagre buildings in which the life-style of the occupants can never be improved. Unfortunately our technology allows us to build meanly at an enormous scale, and to make huge profits in the process.

In such a cultural situation, monuments carry a subversive message, of conspicuous consumption, of lost erudition, of values beyond the mundane. They are reminders of our better selves, our communal responsibilities and of our present slavery to the requirements of the production process. It is no wonder that there is so much pressure to replace them with plastic packs for conveniently processed people.

Notes towards a general theory

It is true that throughout history architects have constantly returned to the simple geometrical shapes, cube, cylinder, sphere, pyramid for inspiration and as a kind of moral imperative. There is something of primal virtue in simplicity and certainly our eyes and minds are constructed to simplify and analyse into primary shapes and solids. We automatically 'correct' complex configurations into simple forms, and primary forms and colours seem to affect us deeply.

At the same time, the human mind has a tendency to elaborate, and to complicate, and it is perhaps no accident that simplicity is always characteristic of early phases of civilizations. The Egyptians built the pyramids at the beginning of their civilization, when the simple social structure allowed an equally simple formula to express it. Later periods in all civilizations tend to floridity and rich luxuriance. Late Roman architecture shares with the Baroque a feeling for complexity, for the grand scale, and it reflects, at the same time, a complex social background. It similarly expresses the contemporary requirements for new and varied building types, for which there was no precedent, or need, in earlier times.

When society changes, so does its architecture; the fanciful and luxuriant Gothic world died under the logic of double entry bookkeeping, and humanism brought architects back to the path of virtue, the elementary solids and noble simplicity. Yet within a hundred years it was all complexity again, and stayed so until the French Revolution and the concomitant austerities of the neo-classic revival.

The recent controversy over the façade of the Tate Gallery illustrates the simplifying, reducing tendencies of our time. A vociferous public protest prevented this outrage

Above left: the existing front
Left: the proposals for the new extension
Above: an accurate and sarcastic comment by Garland in the Daily Telegraph

In effect, the whole of architectural history can be seen as an alternation between ideals of elementary simplicity (virtue) beloved by the theorists and art historians, and periods of tangled complexity, which are always somehow more popular, and challenging, for the practitioners. Each periodic recall to virtue results in the neglect and decay of the buildings of the previous period. Roman temples provided useful columns for Christian churches; Gothic cathedrals caused embarrassment in the age of elegance. Victorian railway stations are equally embarrassing today.

It has taken three generations of architects and critics to establish the modern movement in architecture, and to do so required a fanaticism that determinedly ignored the past. This theoretical drive excused (and continues to excuse) vast areas of inadequate building on grounds of 'modernity' and 'simplicity'. We have quite simply destroyed the past, and our feelings of continuity with the past. No architect under fifty can even think of designing in any other style but 'modern'; none can speak in the dead languages of historical architecture, and very few can even understand what the buildings mean.

Notes towards a general theory

Notes towards a general theory

No generation of architects could have been so isolated from tradition since that of the early Renaissance. While their commitment was to the past, to stones that could be measured, ours is to a misty future. Our thinking is future oriented towards a world of mobility, of instant communications, of temporary, disposable structures, of continuous change and transition. We have to think in terms of vast population increases, of a building programme that must in thirty years build more than everything built in the world to date. We can be sure these buildings will be modern, clean and elementary, because that's the way accountants, and system builders, like it.

In this welter of new buildings, new things, and continual change, all cities will be submerged, and any regional differences ironed out. Already it is possible to travel the world and see only the foyers of Hilton Hotels, to view from your standard bedroom the elementary glass towers of Dallas, or Denver, or London, or Brussels.

In this new cityscape the fragments of the past that remain take on a haunting and poignant value. Even where an isolated church cowers in a canyon on Wall Street it asserts a human value, provides an architectural measure, and a social landmark. It provides the place with a recognizable identity. Even unremarkable buildings serve remarkably in this context, and deserve our love and care.

How much more valuable then are those great monuments of the immediate past that still litter our cities like stranded whales. A vast intelligence and ingenuity was expended on them; their complicated skylines still dominate our cities, though perhaps not for long, for they are mostly without protection.

We have been slow to recognize their tremendous values, in the changed situation of the future city. At present the buildings (such as the Foreign Office or Street's Law Courts in the Strand, London) appear to the inmates to be cramped and uncomfortable, mainly because they are crowded and overused. Their architectural value is obscured by careless maintenance, and by minor irritations on functional grounds. People have changed and the building has not.

In this situation there are many who would like a rapid replacement by something modern. But such a view would take no account of the building's true value, of its place in the city scene and the city's vitality, of its share of a city's invisible tourist earnings. The logical course is to examine the building, refurbish it, and provide the modern services, and to take the pressure off by providing alternative accommodation for the excess population.

Left: Wall Street, New York

The Pool of London. Note the effect of the new development, adjoining the Tower of London, on the grain of the city. Such forms have no capacity for growth and change

By this method the building can be preserved to play its more important role. In the future city we will need monuments, places to visit, to look and wonder at, for this is the purpose of our hard won mobility. In the coming years of mass international transportation, when whole populations will move each summer, the pressure on the older, established monuments will be unbelievable. Already the numbers are vast, and the pleasures of visiting are greatly reduced. This great surge of affluent, leisured visitors must be spread more evenly. Those monuments that now attract only a handful of enthusiasts will one day earn their keep as national treasures, if they can be preserved for a few years more from our short-sighted greed and carelessness.

In the 'twenties, at the beginning of the modern movement, our great men preached purity and simplicity, and forty years later the remaining pioneers are still trotted out by their commercial masters to display their elementary building blocks. In the meantime their simplistic philosophy has, by the magic of modern communications, been externalized in whole cities, and, enshrined in the hearts of bureaucrats all over the world, become an offical dogma. Particularly in planning theory and practice we find elementarism everywhere: single purpose areas (housing estates, factory estates), single purpose buildings (office blocks, apartment blocks), single purpose utilities (roads, pipelines, pylons), all following their own particular routes and dogmas divorced from the total community they are supposed to serve.

If we analyse buildings of before the theoretical watershed, we find their complexity of form supported by complexity of use, as well as a complexity of architectural and symbolic meaning. Buildings were usually combination buildings, containing and subsuming many different functions. Tower Bridge owes its form to its contradictory functions and is enriched by their resolution. In the same way we might be able to enrich our own buildings by re-thinking their programmes to provide a variety of accommodation. And, in fact, where this has occasionally been done an infintely more civilized building has emerged.*

* The German Rathaus or town hall always includes an excellent public restaurant. Early skyscrapers were not quite so concerned with prestige as at present. They always included shops at pavement level. The variety of subsequent food smells is one of the delights of New York.

Left: the Maltings, Snape, an old barn re-structured as an opera house and concert hall for Benjamin Britten by Philip Dowson of Arup Associates
Above: warehouses near New Quay, Liverpool, magnificent buildings in search of a new role.

In effect, complex requirements produce complex buildings. Ours is a society rapidly becoming more and more complicated, yet our buildings are largely impoverished, reflecting very little of our growing needs.

Because all urban tendencies are today towards a spread, suburban growth, we need to create antidotes. In itself, spread cities are not diseased, nor yet are they true cities. Suburbia is a mode like any other, and its social danger is that it separates out the family into an independent unit. Secure with built-in entertainment, the family feeds upon itself and loses social cohesion. The resultant problems of teenage delinquency, middle-aged boredom and old age loneliness are all too familiar to the middle classes, who have lived the suburban life for a generation or two.

These problems of affluence now begin to affect larger and larger numbers of people, and to reach classes singularly unprepared for a non-communal life. Once upon a time the introspective pleasures of life on one's own acre were sought by the educated few, as a distraction from city social life. Today it is almost compulsory for vast numbers of US citizens, whose cities have become too dangerous to live in.*

To create social cohesion requires a great social investment, but it must be done, and soon. To survive, a society, like a person, must grow in proportion; private life and public life are both essential. Our technology has tended to promote private life (the motor car, radio, television), at the expense of the public sector. (Galbraith's dictum 'private affluence and public squalor'.) We need more than we at present realize to build and run baths, theatres, concert halls, museums, art schools. These are the structures needed to balance the factories and housing estates, to create the nuclei around which new cities can grow.

If we look around we find that there are numbers of large, often beautiful buildings waiting for these uses. The best new theatre in London is a converted warehouse; an old engine shed has become a theatre in the round; a Suffolk barn has become an opera house. Warehouses, today of less and less value as distribution methods change, can convert to an infinite number of uses. In this way good buildings can be saved, and we can make necessary social investments in an economical and intelligent way, a way which also grows the invisible earnings of tourism and culture on which we will live in the next century.

---

* Saint Louis, Missouri, in 1969 has seen a murder a day; most big US cities do much better.

Plant a seed to grow a city

We can predict with some confidence, barring the holocaust, that our population and our productivity will rapidly increase. To take a short term view, in say fifteen years, the population of Britain, for example, will increase by five million ($9\frac{1}{2}$%) and productivity by at least 45%, and more likely nearer 80%. With this vast increase in scale (5·3 million people in new dwellings, plus all the necessary schools, shops, hospitals, etc.), we will find the problems of preservation becoming an ever smaller consideration. A mere 100,000 structures are listed as of architectural merit (though this ignores the vast areas of splendid, anonymous building which makes up the matrix of the mature city), and this is a fraction of a single year's production.

Much of the new building will inevitably go into new situations, new towns, expanded old ones, and into the outer regions of the great cities; literally, into the fields.

Once upon a time urban growth was set off by some physical or geographical incident – a river ford, a crossroad, a defendable pass, a sacred place. Today any stretch of productive farmland will do. Services are easily provided. All that is missing is a good reason to build it *there.*

Cities with a good reason grow faster and richer, but, more important, they stay alive beyond the impulse of their initial founding. They are capable of regenerating themselves, repairing their own tissue, through an internal economic and social dynamic.

This is hardly the case with our new towns, our expanded villages, those miles of suburbia tacked on to the already inadequate centres of the great cities. We have built, not cities, but housing estates, factory estates and very little else. These places are financed in the short term, and have the look and feel of temporary accommodation. The inhabitants hope to move on, to follow the economic treadmill that seems to require wage earners to live surrounded by others in the same bracket. In these circumstances the environmental quality can only diminish, as a visit to any older housing estate will show. Successful inhabitants move out; the unsuccessful stay put; the buildings become physically obsolete; the financing system places responsibility on a distant and increasingly bored bureaucracy. Finally it seems there is no alternative but to pull it down and rebuild, thus destroying the few remaining social strands that make the place bearable. In British practice this process should be repeated every forty years. In the USA, perhaps every twenty.

There can never have been a more wasteful mode of growing a town.

Left: banners at Expo 67, Montreal

Plant a seed to grow a city

Plant a seed to grow a city

Yet to subvert the massive bureaucracy and the political dealing that is involved in building a new town is an impossible task. No planner could create an organic growth with every factor against him, with every one of his proposals either a tried and true failure or a risk impossible to contemplate in the circumstances. An impenetrable net of economic constraint, precedent and administrative complexity, hangs over all new city growth. It cannot be conquered.

But, perhaps, just once or twice, it might be outflanked.

To build a new city we need an occasion, a gesture, a meaning. We also need a massive injection of money, over and above the provision of the minimum dwelling stock.

This money is needed to establish the place, to provide the focus and reason for the city; the seed money for its future self-regenerating growth.

Such necessary sums do not figure in the calculations of any country's Treasury. They produce no short term economic return, and thus have no apparent validity.

At least that is so in the case of investment in the apparatus of our daily lives. In other cases, where the accountants are technically at a loss, money is freely available: for aircraft unlikely to fly, for rockets which never leave the pad; for technologies which most scientific opinion considers to be of highly dubious value (such as the Concorde); for prestige in various departments.

Above: wind sculptures and the Gyrotron at Expo 67
Left: air view of the island reclaimed from the St Lawrence river

The British spent £3 million on a pavilion at Montreal's Expo 67, and many other nations spent a good deal more. The benefits, if any, were intangible; yet the Treasury, in this area, accepts the necessity for expenditure, and acknowledges the value of the gesture in promoting our culture and way of life.

To bring this kind of promotional money into the field of environment would make spectacular changes, physically and spiritually. The easiest way might be to promote a world exhibition, to create the heart of a new city. Montreal invested £400 million to produce Expo 67 and at the end of the exhibition had lost £100 million. But the gains are outside this accounting. The city has been restructured: new motorways, a new underground railway, a vast upsurge in economic growth of every kind. The exhibition site itself, reclaimed from the St Lawrence river, is a massive gain. Built in less than three years, Expo 67 could feed, entertain and transport 500,000 visitors a day, the equivalent of the core of a city for three million.

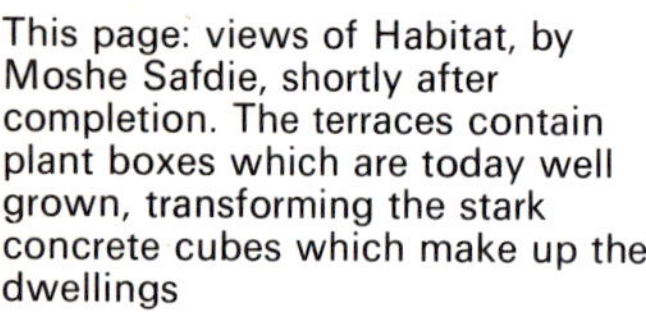

This page: views of Habitat, by Moshe Safdie, shortly after completion. The terraces contain plant boxes which are today well grown, transforming the stark concrete cubes which make up the dwellings

Opposite page, above: the US pavilion at Expo 67, a geodesic dome by Buckminster Fuller
Below: a collage of modern monuments which could form the nucleus of a city centre

Plant a seed to grow a city

It shows a sad lack of foresight that most of the pavilions have now disappeared. Such an investment in infrastructure, roads, services and transport could form the basis of a new city. The pavilions provided by the participating nations could have become very easily the cultural buildings for which new towns wait in vain. It only remains to add the suburbs. In the case of Montreal, Habitat demonstrated the most elegant and sophisticated housing concept in the world, the crystallization of many years of research and opinion from all over the world. There it will probably remain, an interesting demonstration. In a properly co-ordinated investment programme, it would simply keep on growing, recovering its development costs, creating the housing component of the city.

Most world exhibitions provide precisely what is most lacking in new towns; choice, variety and the competitive involvement of great talents – especially the latter. Cities, even new cities, require great buildings, as landmarks, elements of physical identity in a matrix of normality; they are elements of spiritual identity which create the necessary climate of social involvement. Great buildings help to produce great cities, fill citizens with pride, help to subsume private ambition within the collective, because they stand as symbols of the collective.

Marina City, Chicago, B. Goldberg and Associates

Post Office Tower, London, Ministry of Public Buildings and Works

U.S. Pavilion, Expo '67 Buckminster Fuller

Guggenheim Museum, New York, Frank Lloyd Wright

Notre Dame de Ronchamps, Le Corbusier

Habitat, Expo '67, Moshe Safdie

Parking

Parking

Parking

Services

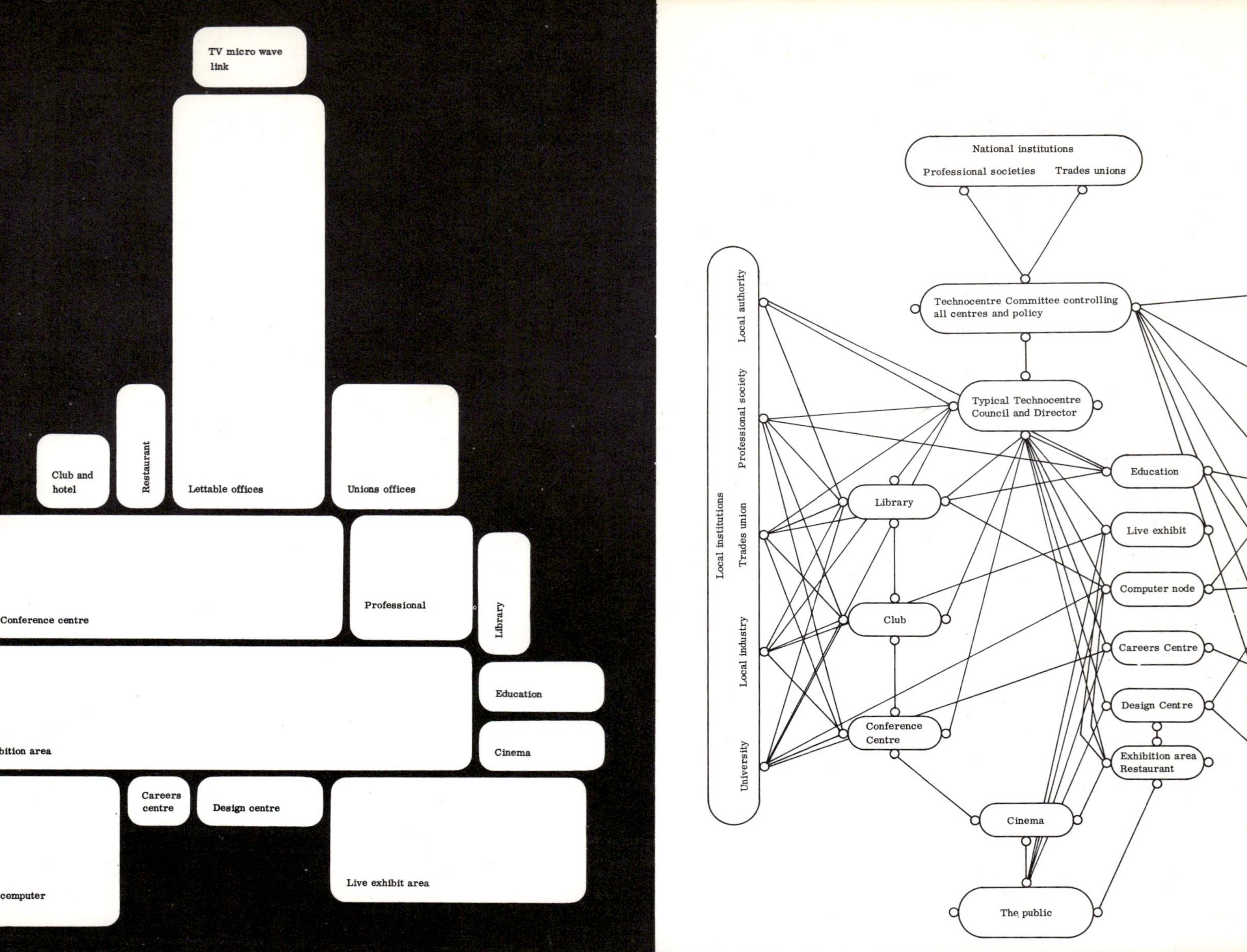
TV micro wave link
Club and hotel
Restaurant
Lettable offices
Unions offices
Conference centre
Professional
Library
Exhibition area
Education
Cinema
Careers centre
Design centre
Live exhibit area
National computer Node
National institutions
Professional societies
Trades unions
Technocentre Committee controlling all centres and policy
Typical Technocentre Council and Director
Local institutions
Local authority
Professional society
Trades union
Local industry
University
Library
Club
Conference Centre
Education
Live exhibit
Computer node
Careers Centre
Design Centre
Exhibition area Restaurant
Cinema
The public
Central Government
Treasury
Transport
Education
Technology
Ministry of Labour
COID

Plant a seed to grow a city

An exhibition is an opportunity to acquire a collection, a demonstration of the best available talent, a marvellous enrichment for daily life, and an investment in tomorrow's tourist trade.

Even if the possibilities of obtaining a major world exhibition are few, there are numbers of other lesser spectacles which might be used in a similar way: the Olympic games, purely national exhibitions and so on. At another level the establishment of a major technical facility produces a fall-out in value which can be capitalized to create a city, rather than a group of housing estates.

For example, a recent proposal by the Ministry of Technology to erect seven 'Technocentres' in Britain could provide a spectacular growth node for a new town or a way of reviving an old one. The technocentres are to consist of the headquarters of engineering professional associations and trades unions, a club, a conference centre linked to the other centres by television, an exhibition, computer centre, a restaurant, cinema and many other elements, all interconnected and each one more or less capable of paying its own way. A healthy subsidy for uneconomic elements was provided by an office building on top. Such a building is a good example of how a multi-use structure can be put together, to fulfil a social necessity, and actually make a profit. Its social role in a city could only encourage growth and raise values in its vicinity. As a centre-piece for a new town its effect would be to attract industry and to establish the elan so conspicuously absent in new development. It would be a monument.

In the end a city depends on its internal energy and self-confidence. The planners' role is to create the situation within which confidence is established and energies released. It is not a problem of negative controls, but of manipulating a vast number of complex interrelated factors, so that investments are made, in a sense, naturally, inevitably; that money is made, rather than saved; that social benefits accrue from private as well as public expenditure.

Above: diagrams of the elements and organization of the Technocentre concept

Questions of identity

Cities that are built or rebuilt within a very short time tend to monotony and repetition in their physical structure. This reflects also their social situation, for the inhabitants of newly built suburbs are usually remarkably homogeneous in their social and economic aspirations. This homogeneity tends to reinforce the original inhabitants' view of themselves, and confirms them in their life styles, prejudices, etc.

This is the case both for new towns and for new suburbs. The older suburbs tend to reflect the values of previous generations and thus are unsatisfactory backgrounds for the life styles of the second generation. The latter seldom feel called upon to defend the thoughts, or buildings of their fathers. This is the problem of the older, emptying, suburbs, and it is part of the larger problem of continuity, and of identity in our culture. With us the cult of the new is a force constantly reiterated by a formidable communications apparatus, which also spreads a cult of conformity.

In the face of continuous pressure to equalize income and opportunity, of being a consumer in a mass society whose choices are both limitless in theory and incredibly restricted in practice, the individual requires constant reassurance as to his unique identity. When religion ceases to offer general consolation or provide a way of communal life within which the individual is both subsumed and sublimated, we must search for alternative psychological supports.

One of the most common is role-playing: the selection of a suitable stereotype and adapting oneself to the inner and outer requirements of the role: hard business man; efficient, or helpless, housewife; tweedy professional; artist; jet setter and so on. The role, thus embodied, becomes the identity of the individual who as time goes by becomes incapable of any other role. It requires a major upheaval, or a war, to change one set of role-players into another set, and of course after the emergency is over the adjustment to a third role is often painful.

In terms of the built environment, or of objects generally, role-playing requires props of various kinds. The ownership of objects is the most important clue to individual identity, and sometimes the game is very subtle indeed. The cuff on a man's coat that actually unbuttons, or the cut of the waistcoat are clues from which one can identify a member of a class or an aspirant to a socially stratified life style.

Left: portrait of Sigismund Malatesta, Lord of Rimini, in the Tempio Malatestiano. This building, by Leon Battista Alberti, provided an irresistible impulse to architectural theory in the Renaissance

The relation to one's tailor is part of the whole range of identity building gambits which go under the general word patronage. To patronize someone is to buy or appropriate a part of their identity

The Chocolate Box
MARKUS COFFEE Co. Ltd.
CONNAUGHT
STREET W2
MARKUS COFFEE

Above: the Tempio Malatestiano, by L. B. Alberti

Left: London houses of about 1840, infinitely discreet and adaptable. The style was derived for middle-class living from the classical tradition re-established by Alberti and Palladio. Within such an integral matrix of building identity is created by subtlety of detail: a bay window, a painted door, a decorative fanlight or balcony railing

and thus reinforce your own. Sigismund Malatesta (1417-68), a minor North Italian war lord, has survived as an individual, and was admired as an intelligent and forceful man in his own time, almost entirely by his patronage of artists and architects. He literally built himself immortality.

In our own time the pressure for equality, and the dominance of evanescent cult figures, as well as the many alternative ways of spending money, have removed most of the temptations to do likewise. The whole cultural climate is organized to immortalize artists (for, as Andy Warhol says, about fifteen minutes) and not their patrons, and conspicuous consumption by the very rich only serves to make them the target of the communications machine.

The possibility of building one's own immortality in the Renaissance way is therefore no longer valid, and our identities must be reinforced in other ways.

The ownership of a work of art, however, if no longer guaranteeing survival after death, is at least a potent indication of one's taste and income level. Surrounding oneself with a collection provides also a constant intellectual stimulus and spiritual refreshment, an observation so true and banal that no one could possibly have written it down for at least a century. A collection is thus a way of establishing identity, and this applies equally to other personal or family objects: books, furniture, and above all the dwelling itself.

Most modern buildings are constructed for anonymous clients. That is, the spaces and surfaces are simple, bland and without personality. It is expected that the occupier will fill the rooms with his own vibrant persona. And, as few people have the talent for this sort of thing, most rooms remain bland, characterless, and are easily given up by their ungrateful owners. In fact, no one wants a room empty of character. The first impulse of the wealthy is to reach for an interior decorator.

An alternative is to commission or to search for a dwelling that in some way externalizes your own requirements for identity. Where you will feel 'at home'; a room, as Christopher Alexander says, with a memory. Such rooms, usually the product of alteration and adaptation, are to be found in old houses, which also carry powerful charges of identity-building imagery. The possession of a great house confers greatness, of an elegant house confers distinction; and it also creates for you a way of life which enables you to be your better self. Though social studies prove that the physical environment is low on the list of factors affecting people, above the middle income bracket it becomes constantly more important. This is the fastest-growing part of the population.

Questions of identity

Questions of identity

In terms of the city, the analogy is very similar. We need to feel at home, but at our best. We need to be surrounded by buildings and objects of value, importance and beauty. Above all, they must be individual, idiosyncratic and preferably unique. The test of a city is its showing in the postcard business. Here the great cities of the modern world, with infinite wealth and productivity, do very badly compared to fifteenth-century Florence or Venice, which had only a fragment of the power and potential.

Identity in the city is only partly a question of scale. A good big monument is splendid, but much of the pleasure of cities comes from small scale invention and complexity: a doorway, a bay window, a spire, an element suddenly seen and exploited in the context of the street. These are fragments, the result of intelligent intervention or forethought, that provide the markers by which one remembers and creates a mental structure of a city. More than the height or size of the glass fronted office block, it is those fragments at street level, or on a skyline, that remain memorable. It is in just these parts that modern building is so helpless, and where buildings of an older tradition are so strong.

Above and left: Victorian building in London 1850-70

A flexible city building system, capable of sustaining a vast range of social levels and economic activities without disrupting the physical structure

Incremental growth provides a lively visual pattern within an accepted harmony of scale

It is these elements which can be seized upon to bolster both a community and an individual identity. Old buildings carry overtones of meaning, some now only very crudely recognizable to us. The architectural vocabulary was capable of many moods, grave and gay, through which we can still be touched. To recognize the language, and the players, to be able to see the jokes, is the richest pleasure of living in cities; to play the game is in itself a mode of establishing identity.

Tentative conclusions

Tentative conclusions

The magic of cities: romantic towers and gloomy chasms of New York; human contacts and associations that conceal much incidental squalor. These social interchanges, becoming outmoded by developments in technology and methods of distribution, need to be recognized and valued for their therapeutic properties. Shopping, once a daily necessity, now becomes a social pleasure, and requires suitable surroundings

In this discussion there can be no conclusions. We are truly in a state of rapid change in social and technical conditions; the very nature of our society is being transformed through a technology which is both liberating and oppressive. The disappearance of poverty and the prospect of the good life for all brings us squarely to the consideration of what the good life consists. Most of the products of the high culture of the past, the buildings, the paintings and sculptures, were intended for a tiny minority and they tend to be overwhelmed by large numbers of visitors. The same can be said of the countryside, the wild high places, the lonely beaches. They cannot and must not be denied the affluent masses, and they are easily destroyed by more intensive use.

The preservation of good things begins now to be more or less accepted as essential to our continued existence, but we have hardly begun to make enough good things for our own time; and we have been slow to realize how valuable and necessary is our inheritance. By making the gestures of commonality, our ancestors set up the markers of human progress. Unnecessary gestures, expensive and impractical. Yet these are the very objects we use our new found affluence to visit. If we are to civilize a mass society we must learn to spend, to live a little, to be as free with life as we are prodigal with death.

The greater part of the good life is freedom: to choose, to talk, to argue, to play and to work, and the widest choices and the best talk are found in cities. There is a magic in human association, in congregation, and in diversity. Only by contact and discussion with our peers do we reaffirm our humanity, discover our own thoughts. By argument and association we retain our dearly-bought liberties.

By their form cities promote or retard this growth of choices: their richness and variety are directly related to land values, access methods and architectural intention. For the visitor the city unfolds another magic; the magic of memory and association, of dreams revisited, the counterpoint of past and present. The romance of cities: New York from Brooklyn Bridge, the towers bloodied in the evening sun; the Thames at twilight, the bridges, the muddy shore and ebbing tide; the slowly waking lights, the spires and the great dome of St Paul; cities by night, lonely walks through echoing, haunted streets; in early morning, the buildings washed with gold. Everyone carries these images in his heart, images of power and complexity, and beside them our plans look thin and amateurish.

Why is it impossible to rebuild in the city without making a desert? Perhaps because we have not stated the problem correctly. We have been concerned only with logic and economy, virtues

STAFF
EMPLOYMEN
RICHARDS
RICHARDS
& Co LIMITED
LOANS
152 J. LYONS & Co Ld 152
ARLEQUIN

The small scale incremental growth of old cities provided an opportunity for a contribution by the individual owner or architect. Within a restricted street frontage all architectural problems can be resolved, and the restrictions themselves provide a stimulus to good design

Above: a thirteenth-century view of Florence
Left: Fenchurch Street, London

admirable in engineers and accountants, but hardly adequate as a base for a culture, or for the good life. A concern for the minimum produces nothing but the minimum.

In this book I have tried to put forward a logic of social need, and a more complex logic of individual and communal identity as a theoretical base for city design. A methodology founded on those premises would result in smaller scale development, based on actual need and not on purely speculative profit. It would avoid comprehensive development which does not allow the maximum of individual commitment and involvement. It would eschew the control of form by means of an arbitrary geometry, and use instead a system of clues derived from the existing environment: compatible heights, rhythms and fenestration. It would encourage the widest possible variety, and flexibility, of use, so that the activities concerned can grow and change without destroying the buildings.*

Such a system would allow a city to grow, but not to explode; a street to develop and change, but avoid excessive growth or decay; produce a consistent variety, and avoid a monotonous consistency.

Within this more complex logic there must be a place for the illogical, irrational object or building. We know little of the mechanisms of human behaviour, but there is in all of us a romantic love of the absurd, the unnecessary, the gilt on the gingerbread, which makes life not just bearable, but positively astonishing and marvellous, super-real.

Many remarkable buildings exist all round us, invisible under a shroud of grime and familiarity. Their rediscovery will give us both profit and pleasure, and their civilizing influence may help to counteract our present excesses. In the context of our cities even a third rate old building becomes a masterpiece when seen beside a modern commercial development.

We need those monuments, all of them, and many, many more.

* The experience with Georgian houses in London or brownstones in New York is especially instructive. They convert readily to flats, hotels, offices or studios without losing their original qualities, and often gain by the change.

Appendix 1

Appendix 1
Tower Bridge: vital statistics

Above: detail of the opening span
Left: the works at Tower Bridge, 24th September, 1892

The bridge consists of two main towers, the river piers, and two smaller towers on the shore abutments, from which the suspension chains of the shore spans are supported. The opening span, with the two bascules pivoting at the face of the river piers, is 200 feet. The clear width of the shore spans is 270 feet. The bascules rise to a vertical position, leaving a clear 141 feet above high water level to the underside of the high level footways.

The headway of the shore spans is between 20 feet at the south abutment, and 23 feet at the north abutment and 27 feet at the river piers. The central span headway is 30 feet with the bridge down. The total length of the bridge is 940 feet; the approaches are 1,260 feet on the north side and 780 feet on the south side. The width between parapets is 60 feet, except across the opening span, where it is 49 feet.

Each of the river towers consists of four octagonal steel columns, 119 feet 6 inches high and 5 feet 9 inches across, braced by three sets of girders, from which the granite cladding is hung. The columns are elaborately stiffened and enlarged towards the bases, which are 14 feet between faces of the octagon, and rest on a granite bed 16 feet square and 3 feet thick. The bed consists of four stones, each 8 feet square, and this rests on engineering blue brickwork. The bases are hollow to contain the bridge machinery and are faced with finely cut granite.

Each tower contains two hydraulic lifts, capable of accommodating twenty-five passengers, as well as two flights of stairs. These lifts were for the pedestrians who would have to wait for the bridge to be lowered. One of the conditions imposed on the designers by the Thames Conservancy was that the bridge should be open for two hours at high water, so making this elaborate provision of lifts and high level walkways necessary. As the bridge opens and closes very efficiently in less than six minutes, they have never been used.

The high level ties, linking the two halves of the bridge together, are combined with the high level walkways and also carry the high pressure water pipes from the south pier to the north. The ties are rigid chains, made up of riveted steel plates 1 inch thick, and are connected over rockers on the main columns to the suspension chains to the shore towers. Since April 1961 the load on the ties has been transferred to 2 inch diameter lock coil steel cables suspended from the main top pins at the head of the shore span chains. The suspension chains in the bridge are rigid, girder-like structures, capable of acting in compression as well as tension, and stiffened to take up and distribute eccentric loadings.

The shore spans are hung from the suspension chains by 6 inch diameter rods at 18 foot centres, and consist of fifteen girders 3 feet 3 inches deep. Between these are longitudinal girders at 7 foot 6 inch intervals, supporting steel troughs $\frac{3}{8}$ inch thick and 6 inches deep, which in turn are covered with coke breeze lightweight concrete and wood blocks, now asphalted over. In the pavements are run water and gas mains and the hydraulic-pressure pipes.

From the shore towers anchor ties are taken deep in the abutments to girders bedded in concrete. The ties are box girders; they have a span of 80 feet and carry a tension of 1,000 tons.

Appendix 1

MAIN
PIVOT
PINIONS
ROAD GIRDER
BEARING
GIRDER
TOOTHED SECTOR
100'0"
T.H.W.

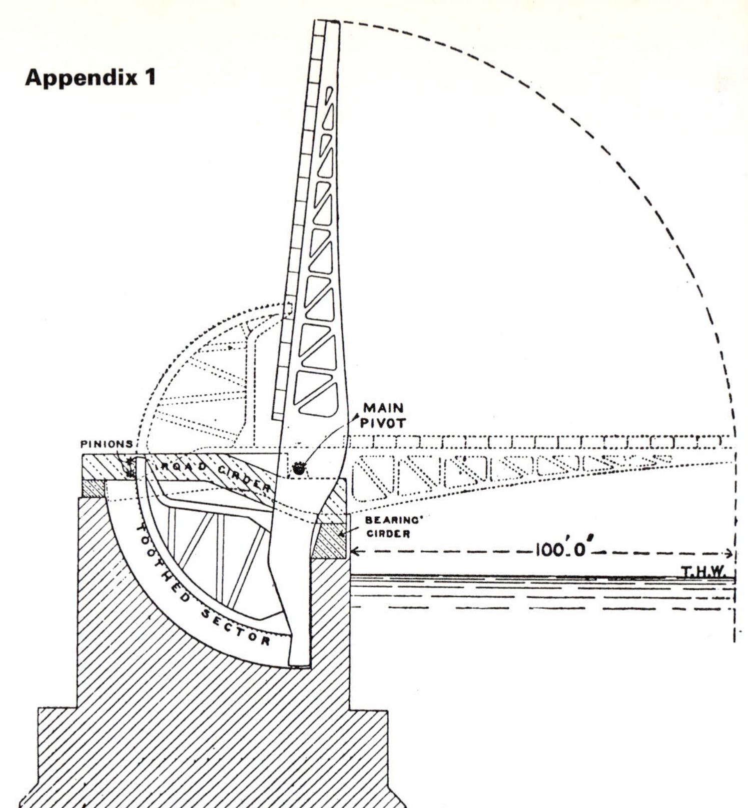

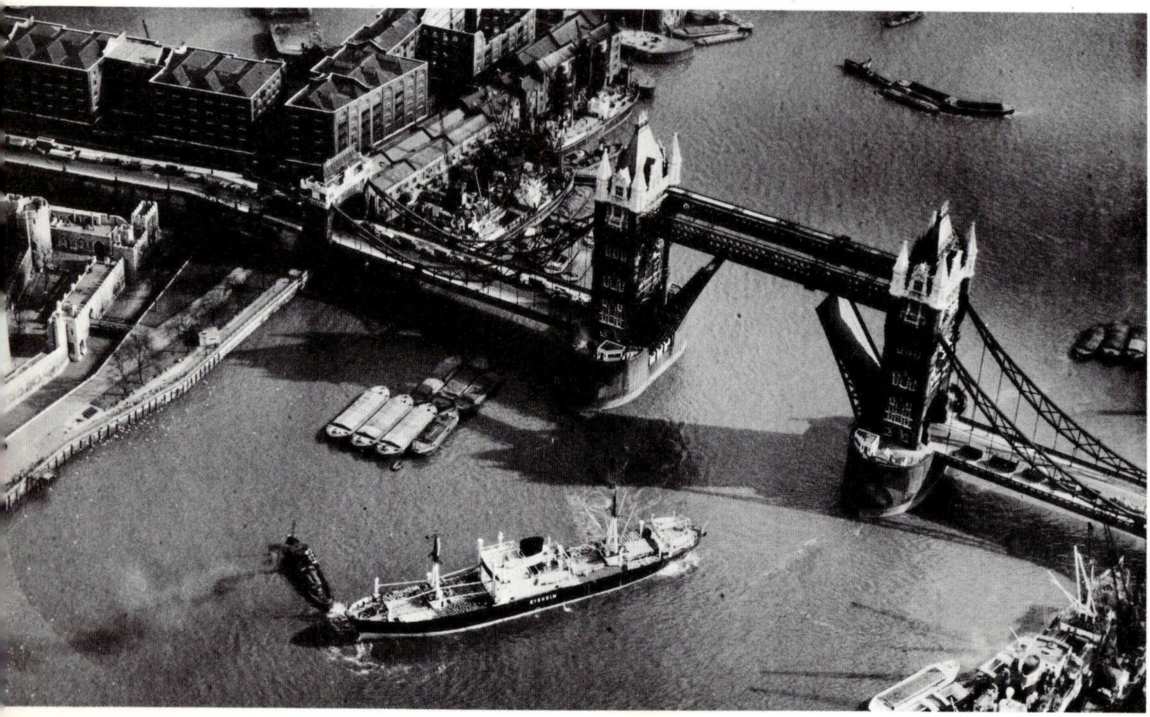

Appendix 1

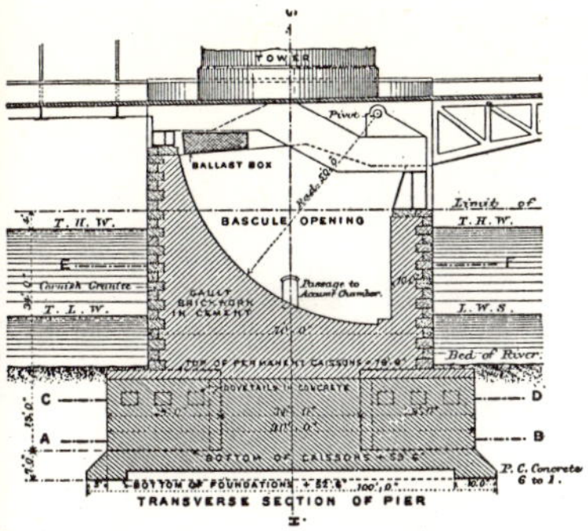

Above: a section through the pier showing the foundations, which are 26 feet below the river bed
Left: diagram of the bascules showing the principal dimensions
Below left: airview of the bascules in action
Below: engineering detail of the bascule chamber

The opening span is one of the mechanical marvels of the nineteenth century. Each bascule consists of four main girders projecting 100 feet over the water and extending 62 feet 6 inches back into the towers. They are 13 feet 6 inches apart, with transverse girders at 12 foot intervals; small transverse and longitudinal girders between these subdivide the floor into spaces 3 feet × 3 feet 6 inches, which are covered with domed floor plates $\frac{3}{8}$ inch thick. On this steel base are shaped timbers and a creosoted pine block road surface laid in asphalt.

The pivot for the span is 13 feet 3 inches inside the face of the pier, so that the underside of the soffit lines with the pier to provide the 200 foot clear opening. The rear ends of the girders rotate down within the bascule chamber. They are connected with transverse girders and loaded with some 365 tons of ballast, mostly lead.

The pivot itself is a shaft of forged steel, 21 inches diameter and 48 feet long, on roller bearings, supported by shaped fixed girders resting on the main tower walls. The total weight on the pivot is 1,070 tons.

The space between the opening leaves at the centre of the bridge varies between $\frac{3}{4}$ inch and $1\frac{3}{4}$ inches, according to temperature. When the bridge was asphalted it was discovered that it expanded rather more than the original calculation and it is now necessary to water the roadway on very hot days to shrink it to size.

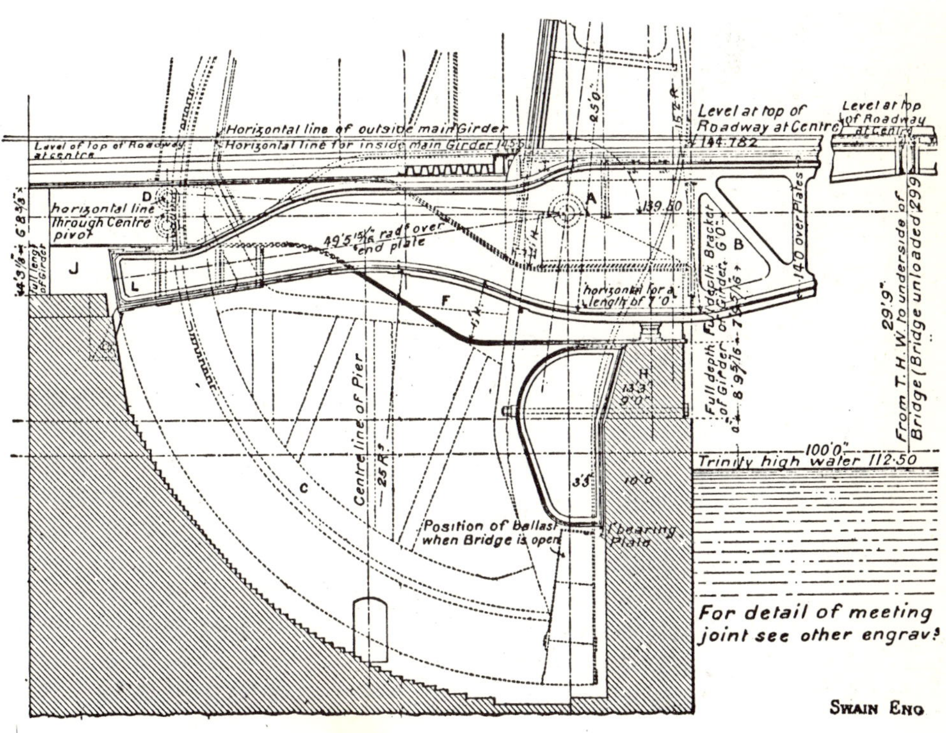

Appendix 1

CENTRE of GRAVITY
CENTRE of GRAVITY
162 3"
49 6"
112 9"
MAIN PIVOT
12 9"
BALLAST
32 9"
48 0"
621 TONS
424 TONS
T.H.W.
100 0"

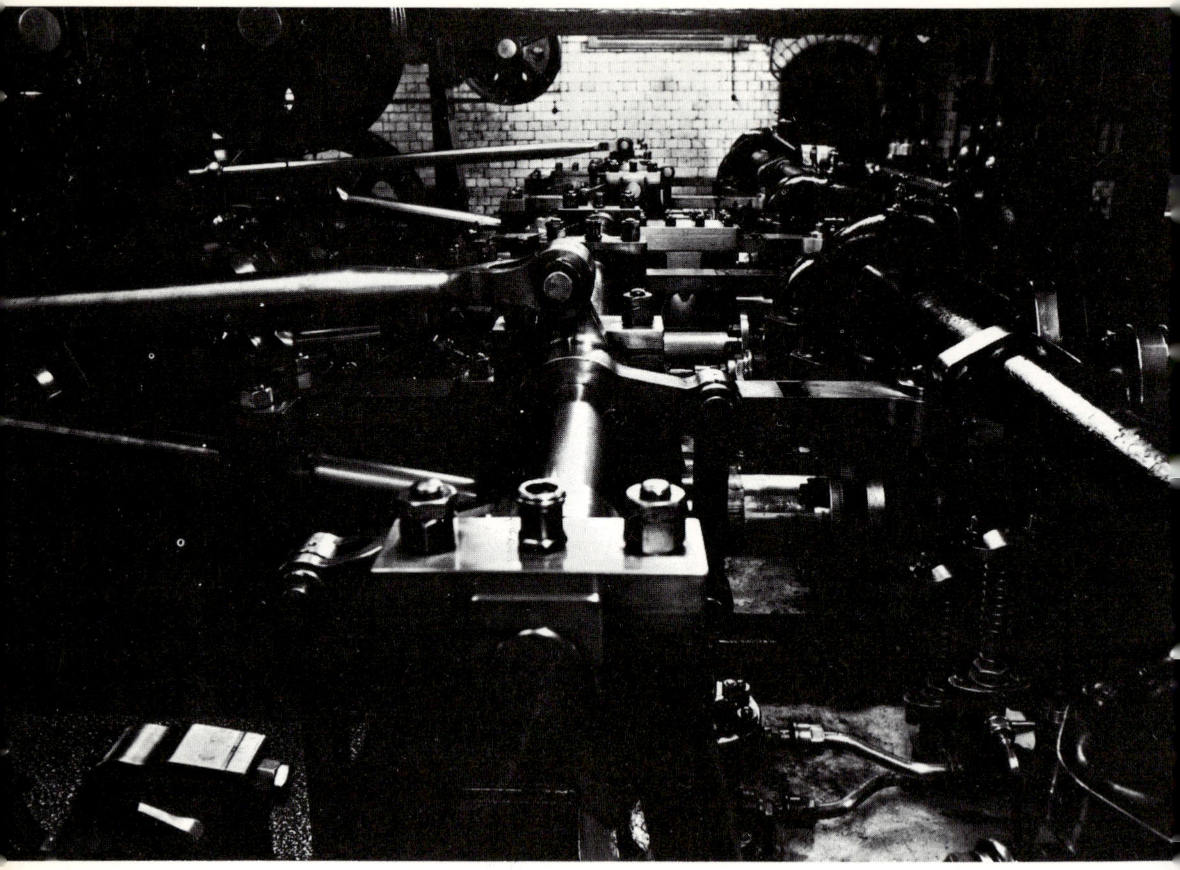

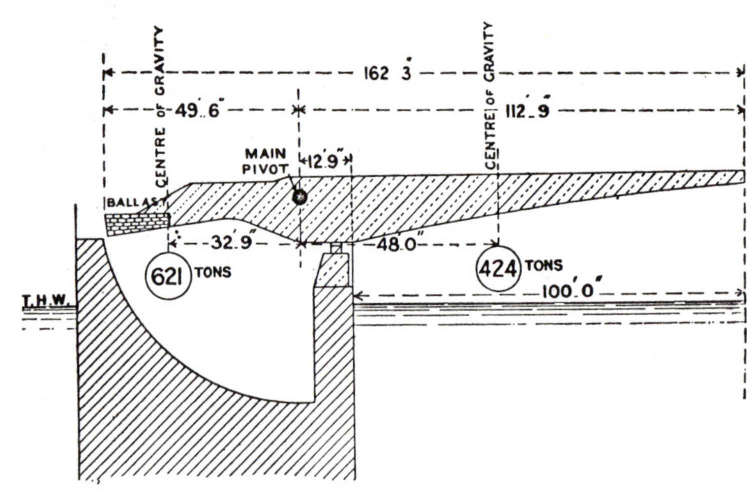

Appendix 1

Above and left: details of the hydraulic engines inside the river towers
Below left: diagram of the loads on the bascule
Below: diagram showing the principle of the accumulator, which provides the hydraulic power for the bridge

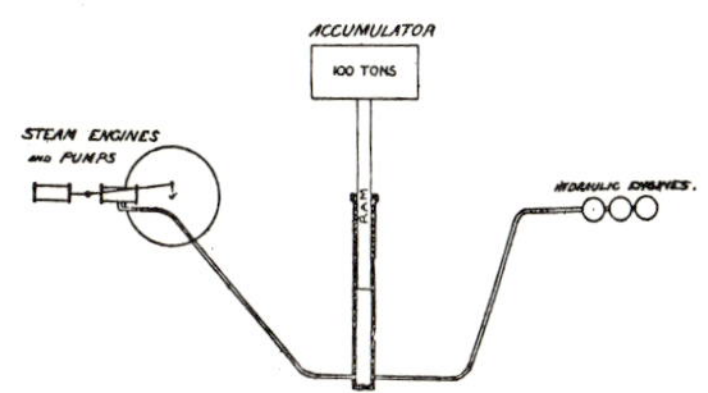

When the south leaf was tested it was found that with a full loading of 112 pounds per square foot the deflection at the end of the span was only $1\frac{3}{8}$ inches.

Because of the Board of Trade requirements, the engines and mechanical provision are generally excessive. The discussion at the Institution of Engineers, at the presentation of the bridge to the profession, was astonishingly free and acidulous on the subject. It was pointed out that hydraulic engines wear out very quickly; that the power required was only a fraction of that provided; and in any case the engines were of an old-fashioned type. The over-provision has, however, meant that the machinery is never under stress; adequate power is always available, and this has certainly been a considerable factor in the bridge's faultless performance for nearly seventy-five years.

The machine house for the boilers and engines is placed under the roadway on the Surrey side of the bridge. The steam engines pump water into four accumulators, one on each side of the main towers and a main accumulator in its own house on the south bank. An accumulator consists of a cylinder, containing a plunger, with a heavy weight on top. Water pumped into the cylinder raises the plunger, which then keeps the water under pressure of 700 pounds per square inch until it is required to move something. It is a simple system, but awesome at this scale.

The hydraulic mains are remarkably flexible and versatile. Apart from the main functions of powering the bascules and lifts, the pressure is used for delivering water to the fire mains in the towers, and to the officers' quarters. The bascules are locked by hydraulic power, which also works the over run buffers deep within the bascule chambers, the signals and all the complex control and safety gear.

The tower accumulators consist of plungers 22 inches in diameter, with a stroke of 18 feet; the main accumulator tower houses two cylinders 20 inches in diameter with a stroke of 35 feet.

Within each river pier are two engine sets, one on either side, and each capable of driving the bascules. Each set contains two engines, a small one for normal opening and a large one for stormy weather. For very bad weather both together provide the power to raise the bridge against a wind pressure of 56 pounds per square foot.

The engines act on the bascules through gearing to rotate spur wheels on the toothed racks bolted to quadrants on the outside moving girders. The engines have three fixed single acting cylinders with plungers $8\frac{1}{2}$ inches in diameter and 27 inch stroke in the larger engine, and $7\frac{1}{2}$ inch diameter and 24 inch stroke in the smaller. The plungers work through exquisitely shaped connecting rods to crank shafts which revolve the gearing. There are a great many refinements and safety provisions: brakes, automatic stopping gear, hydraulic buffers for the counter balance, locking gear to secure the opening span in position, all worked by the ubiquitous hydraulic system.

Appendix 1

Appendix 1

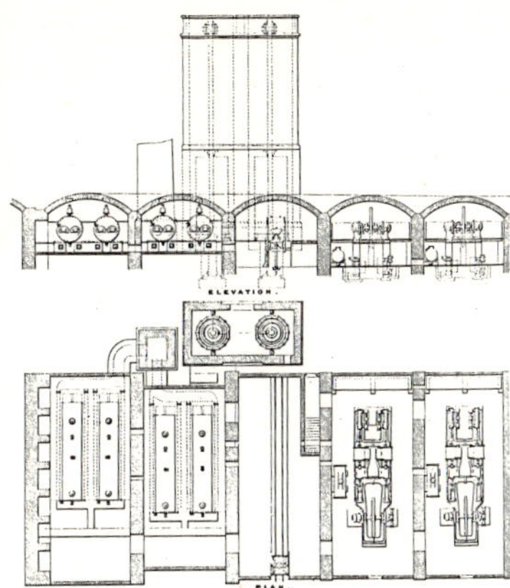

Above: plan and section through the south approach road showing the boilers, coal store and pumps, and the accumulators
Left: the Watt governor, the invention which prototyped the concept of feed-back by which a machine's performance can be automatically regulated, on one of the great steam engines.

Each bascule is normally raised by one engine, the other three being in gear and running idle, the water circulating through their cylinders and valves. Power can thus be varied, or the engine changed, or an engine brought into action at the opposite side of the pier.

Those water pipes which work the centre span locking bolts and other safety gear are necessarily exposed, and in the winter a mixture of glycerine and water, forming a small system of its own, is used to prevent freezing.

The hydraulic power for the bridge is generated in the arches under the south access road.

Here the two original engines are by Sir W. G. Armstrong & Co., Ltd, and are double tandem compound surface-condensing steam engines, each of 360 IPH, having high pressure cylinders 19¾ inches diameter, low pressure cylinders 37 inches diameter, force pumps 7¾ inches diameter and a stroke of 38 inches. One of these engines is enough, more than enough, to power the bridge. A third smaller engine was installed in 1958, which now relieves the two great engines. The latter are in perfect condition, beautifully painted and maintained, and should truly be one of the sights of London. Steam is supplied by four boilers 7 feet 6 inches in diameter and 30 feet long, producing a pressure of 85 pounds per square inch. Two boilers are generally in use, the others being kept in reserve.

The original coal supply system, with hydraulic cranes for unloading from barges and lifts is now unused, and coal is delivered by road. The result is untidy and the surroundings are anyway congested by motor vehicles. If the boilers could be converted to gas or oil, the whole area might be cleaned up and made accessible to the public. This idea is explored in the chapter on 'The social connection'.

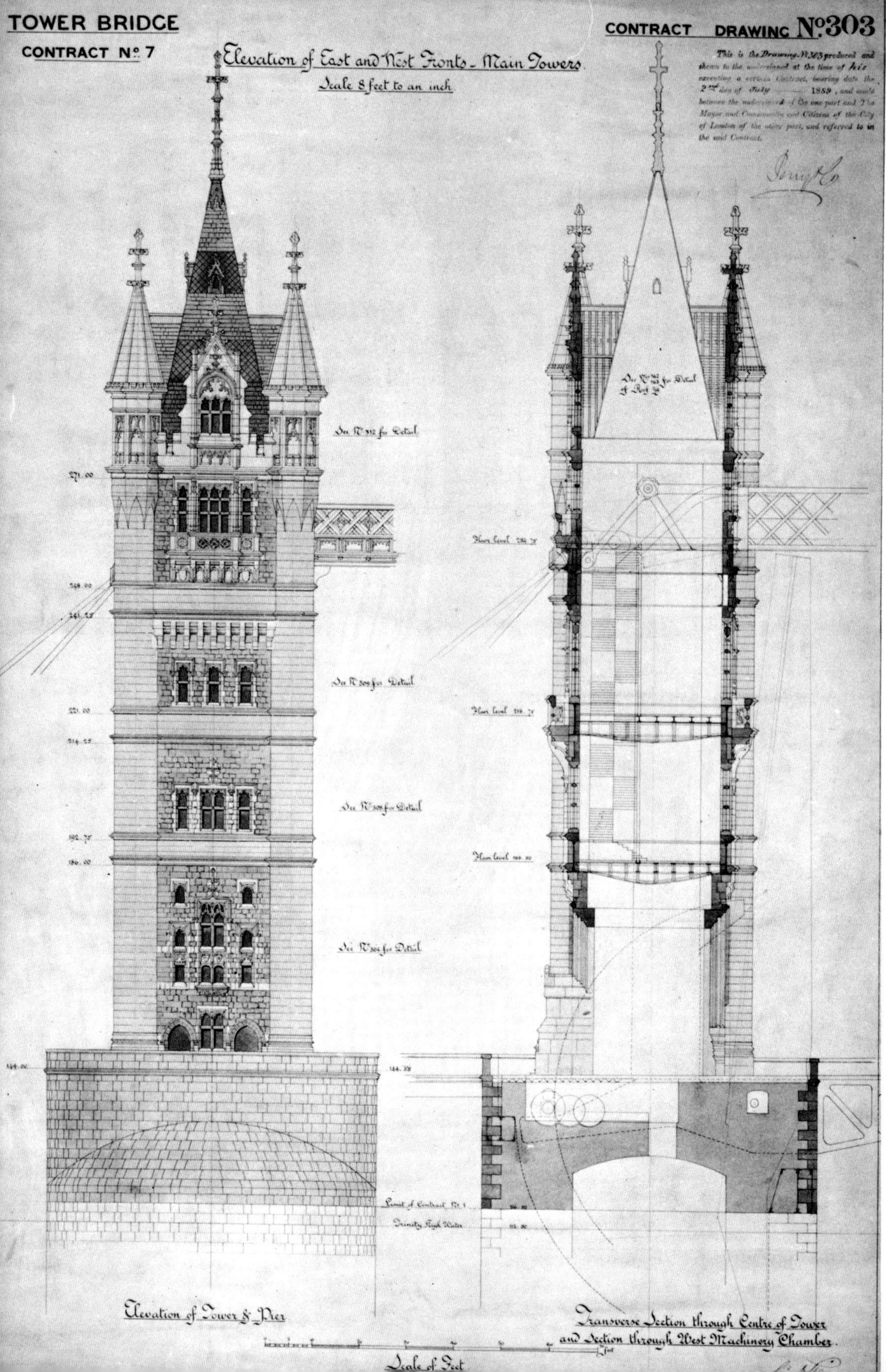
TOWER BRIDGE
CONTRACT No. 7
Elevation of East and West Fronts – Main Towers
Scale 8 feet to an inch
CONTRACT DRAWING No. 303
This is the Drawing No 303 produced and
See No 312 for Detail
See No 309 for Detail
See No 308 for Detail
See No 304 for Detail
Floor level
Limit of Contract No. 1
Trinity High Water
Elevation of Tower & Pier
Transverse Section through Centre of Tower
and Section through West Machinery Chamber
Scale of Feet

Appendix 2
A structural appreciation by Edmund Happold

The structure of Tower Bridge is unusual. The bridge is a continuous one consisting of a pair of bascule leaves for the centre span, two suspension bridges for the shore spans, and two high level footways connecting the chains for the suspended spans over the centre. The main vertical features consist of two main towers on river piers and two smaller towers on shore abutments. The main towers are designed as vertical cantilevers from the piers. They consist of a skeleton of steelwork covered with a facing of stone. The opening span, between the two main towers, consists of two bascules pivoted near the faces of the piers like drawbridges, so that when they are raised ships can pass through the bridge. The bascules are counterbalanced within the tower piers, and the reactions caused by raising and lowering are taken directly to the riverbed through the piers.

Across the towers, from shore to shore, runs the tie system from which the shore spans are hung. This system is a series of rigid links, pinned at the joints and carried over the towers on rollers. The rigidity of the links varies; where the shore spans are carried from them on hangers the links are trussed to deal with unequal loading; where no weight is carried straight rods will do. The linkage system ensures that any settlement of the foundations of the piers would not affect the structure. It also means that the system is a mechanism and a load on one shore span could raise the other one. To reduce this movement an extra frame was inserted in the parapet on the Surrey side between the shore tower and the intersection of the two links.

The high level links extend from main tower to main tower and are hung from the top beams of the outer footway girders. The ends of these footway girders are cantilevers, tied back to the towers, with independent middle girders supported from their ends.

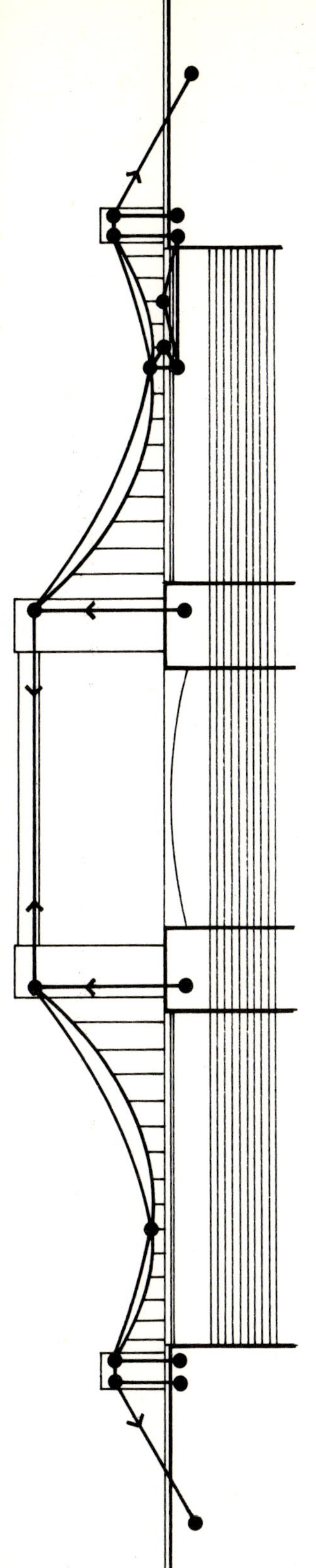

Diagram of the suspension spans showing the linkage system

This design, a modification of that originally proposed by the City Architect, Sir Horace Jones, was carried out by Sir John Wolfe Barry. The Resident Engineer, Mr G. E. W. Cruttwell, presented a paper on the bridge to the Institution of Civil Engineers in 1896. Sir John was President of the Institution at the time and so took the chair. During the discussion which followed this paper several engineers cast doubts on the quality of the solution with a candour which would certainly cause deep offence if it happened today. The main question was whether there was justification for 'planting down in the middle of the fairway of the River Thames two impediments which bore such a large ratio to the total width of the stream'. Why could there not be a single span? Subsidiary questions were asked as to why a suspension system was required for the shore spans; could they not be lattice girders? Could a stiffening truss in the parapet have obviated the need for the stiffening linkage on the Surrey side? The biggest question of all was implied and answered several times, though never asked. Why have high level footways, which were never needed?

Sir John Wolfe Barry took the full opportunity of being chairman to answer his critics. He claimed that at the time of the initial design there was no gain in a single span as, in those days, there were two continuous lines of ships moored 100 feet from the centre line down the Thames, and the river traffic passed down the centre. Piers therefore caused no obstruction; three spans were more economic and also provided, in the piers, space for the lifting

Appendix 2

Roof
Roof Landing
High Level tie
Roller bearings
Top landing
Wind bracing
Middle land[g]
First land[g]
Columns
Suspension Bods
Quad[t]
Long Segment Chain
Short Segment Chain
Horizontal links
Roller bearings
Land tie
Abutm[t] Columns
Column base
Fixed Girder
Girder J
Movable Girders
Girder H
Cantilevers
T. H. W.
270'0"
70'0"
North Abutment
North Pier
Short Segment
Long Segment
Top of Parapet
Level of Roadway at Centre
Line of Headway Limit
It is very important that the intersection of these 2 lines should meet in this line
Surrey Abutment
1⅛ Rivets in Joints
Top of Parapet
1⅛ Rivets in Coverplates
1" Coverplates
1" Rivet
Distance pieces
1" Bolts
1⅛ Bolts
½ Springy plates to bear hard against L & packing
1" Plate
¾ Plate
¾ Web
1" Bolts
Cross Section at F.F.
Detail of Parapet elsewhere
Surface of Fotway
1¼ Bolts
Line of Headway Limit
½ Spring plates to bear hard against L & pack[g]
Cross Section at H H
Surface of Footway
⅞ Rivets
1" Coverplate
9'0
5 N[os] 1" Plates 1'3" wide
"The Engineer"
Swain Eng.

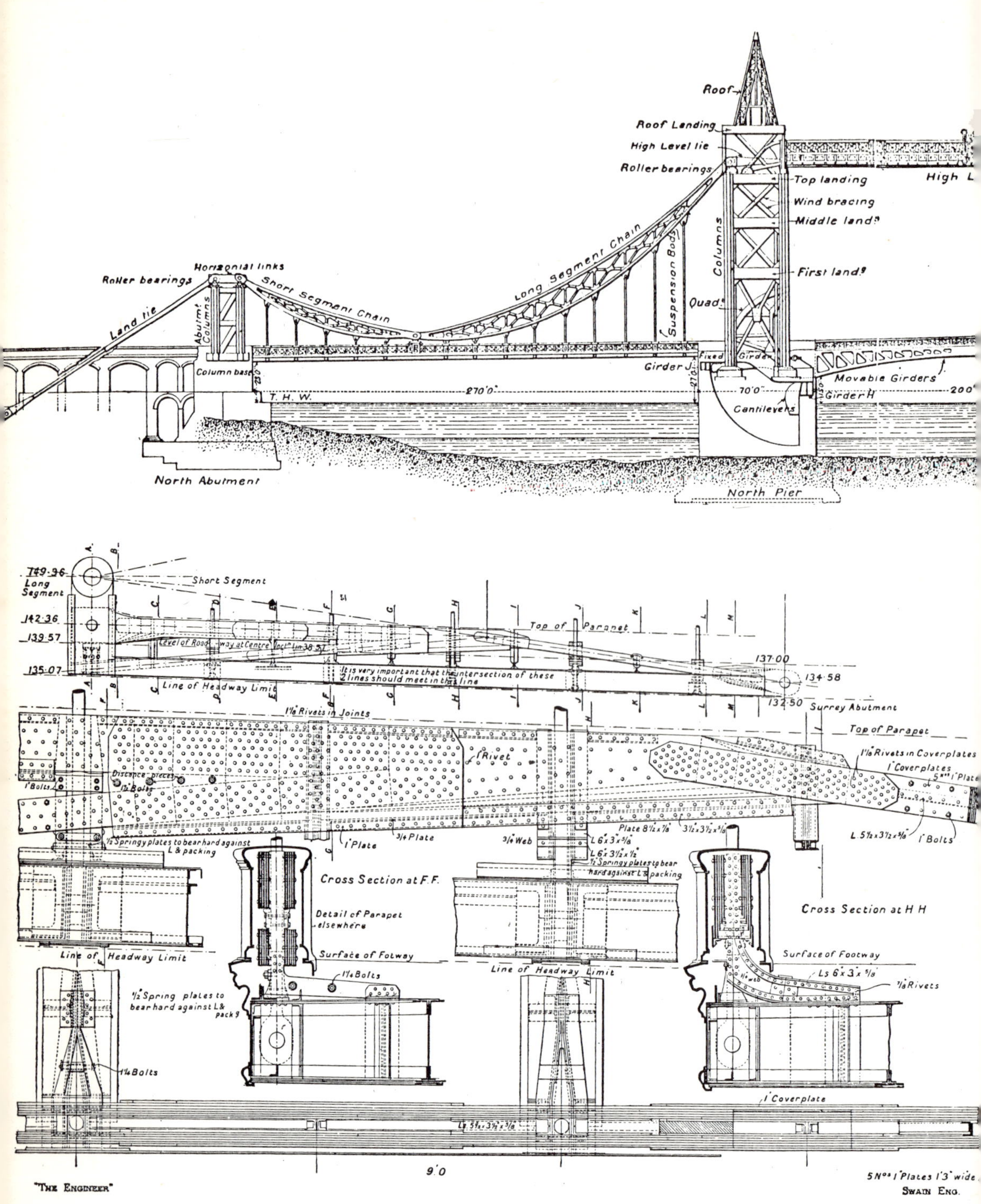

Appendix 2

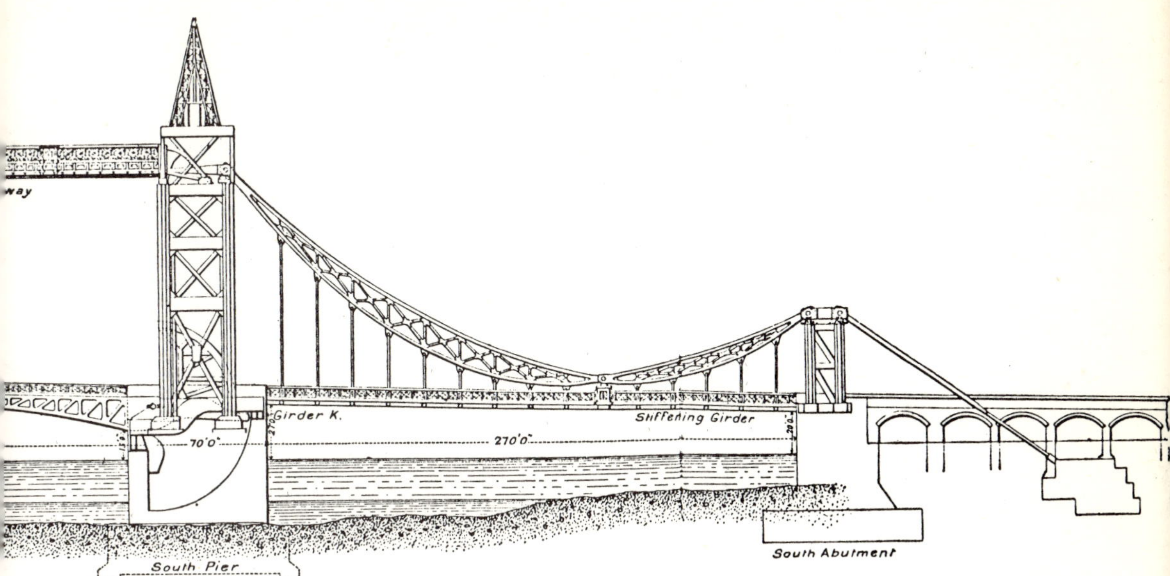

machinery for the bascules which would have been difficult to allow for in the bottom boom of a single span bridge. He also said that when they had carried out the design, the Thames Conservancy had very large powers as to the times of opening the bridge and had insisted that it would be necessary to keep the bridge open for ships for two hours at every high water. This requirement had never been enforced, largely due to the bridge machinery's ability to raise and lower the bridge in three to six minutes, but it led to the provision of two towers and high level walkways which, in turn, led to the adoption of the suspension principle for the side spans.

Top: a section showing the arrangement of the steelwork
Above: the link in the suspension span on the Surrey side
Left: detail of the stiffening girder on the Surrey span

Here is probably the main criticism of the design. If machinery is put in to enable the bridge to be raised and lowered in under six minutes, why did the engineers go to the enormous expense of providing the tall towers and the high level footways? Not only that, but it led the designers, in trying to utilize the towers further, to offend engineering manners by mixing structural systems of cantilever bascules and suspended side spans. Good engineering design, like good architecture, has a literacy. Many structural systems can be chosen but they should never be mixed. Disorder results. Perhaps the designer fell into the same trap as many architects, that of having an emotional idea and insisting on building it, rather than evaluating alternatives and dispassionately selecting the optimum. Alternatively he fell into the trap many engineers do, that of not questioning the correctness of the limitations set on the design.

It is interesting to speculate what form the bridge would have taken if the footbridges had not been provided. Probably it would have been a swing bridge with double cantilevers turning on the piers. If so the machinery required would have been smaller and the piers correspondingly so. Certainly though it would have been less dominating and its monumental character, such a symbol to the world, have been lost.

Appendix 2

Criticism of the overall engineering concept should not be allowed to detract from the clarity of understanding of some of the detailing. For example, the main towers consist of a skeleton of steelwork covered with a facing of granite and Portland Stone, and backed with brickwork on the inside faces. There is a risk of bearing failure under the steel columns, which carry the whole weight of the towers together with the footways and part of the suspension chains and their loads. To obviate this risk, the designer provided layers of canvas and red lead between the granite pier and the base of the steelwork, in order to obtain a uniform bearing over the whole surface. To provide for expansion and contraction the columns were wrapped with oiled canvas to prevent the adhesion of the cement to the steelwork.

These columns were delivered in small pieces and erected by cranes on the piers. As load came on the columns there was a danger that the cross bracing would slacken and so the rivet holes at one end of the cross bracings were drilled sufficiently short of the corresponding holes in the columns to allow for any subsequent column contraction. The bracing ties were then heated by gas jets and, on expansion, riveted up. These induced stresses in the ties had been checked and subsequent loading only reduced them.

Certainly the designer was right to articulate the bridge. One of the piers of the then new London Bridge had subsided 1½ inches when the load arrived on the foundations.

The scale of such a bridge was large for those days and the quality of detailing is perhaps best illustrated by how little trouble the bridge has given since its erection. The designer could have fallen into many traps. Certainly he felt responsible to the future. The collapse of the Tay Bridge had caused the Board of Trade to insist that bridges were designed for a wind load of 56 pounds per square foot. Sir John realized that the bascules provided a wind gauge larger than any before. By putting gauges in the machinery rooms they could record the amount and pressure of water used in each operation against all winds from whatever direction. He placed ordinary wind gauges on the high parts of the bridge. Experiments such as these, by many engineers, have led to the safe but economical wind design pressures of today.

Bibliography

Architectural history is well catered for in most libraries and a growing number of books deal with the increasingly respectable nineteenth century. Most of the earlier productions are apologetic, such as H.-R. Hitchcock's invaluable compendium, which searches for clues to validate the official history of modern architecture; others such as Robert Furneaux Jordan's *Victorian Architecture* find the subject thoroughly distasteful. Even a pioneering early work such as Kenneth Clark's *Gothic Revival* is somewhat lukewarm. In particular there is a chronic shortage of detailed study on such great men as Charles Garnier, Viollet-le-Duc, de Baudat, Guimard, Horta, Scott or Waterhouse, and the whole high Victorian period.

However, the point of this book is not to point to the academic fascination of a great era, but to explore the value of its monuments in the context of the present. Here there is even less guidance. Most current writing is simple complaint, or outrage at yet another cultural casualty. The most agonizing howl is Alison and Peter Smithson's dirge for the Euston Arch.

Sigfried Giedion *Space Time and Architecture* Oxford University Press, 1968; Harvard University Press 1954

Kenneth Clark *The Gothic Revival* 1928. Penguin books, Harmondsworth, 1962

Henry-Russell Hitchcock *Architecture Nineteenth and Twentieth Centuries* Penguin books, Harmondsworth, 1958. It includes a remarkably comprehensive bibliography.

Nikolaus Pevsner *Pioneers of Modern Design* 1936. Penguin books, Harmondsworth, 1960

Nikolaus Pevsner *Buildings of England* innumerable volumes since 1951. Penguin books, Harmondsworth

Pamela Ward, editor *Conservation and Development in Historic Towns and Cities,* Oriel, Newcastle upon Tyne, 1968

Lawrence Halprin *New York New York* HUD & NY Housing and Development Administration, 1968

The Regional Plan Association, New York, have published several valuable reports which bear indirectly on this study, and which explore the possibilities of development control in the context of the US economy.

Lewis Mumford *The Brown Decades* Constable, London, 1958; Dover, New York, 1955

Vincent J. Scully *The Shingle Style* Yale University Press, 1955

Reyner Banham *The Architecture of the Well-tempered Environment* Architectural Press, London, 1969. An attempt to find the history of modern architecture not in style but in nineteenth century technology.

Alison and Peter Smithson *The Euston Arch* Thames & Hudson, London, 1968

Giancarlo de Carlo *Urbino* Marsilio Editore, Padua, 1966. Study and intelligent plan for the Italian hill city

Colin Buchanan *Traffic in Towns* HMSO, London, 1963

Christopher Tunnard and Boris Pushkarev *Man-made America* Yale University Press, 1963

The editors of *Fortune: The Exploding Metropolis* Doubleday, New York, 1958.

Bibliography

William H. Whyte *The Last Landscape* Doubleday, New York, 1968. A critically important book on the effects of the move to suburbia and a basic text on how to control development.

Jane Jacobs *The Death and Life of Great American Cities* Cape, London, 1962; Random House, New York, 1961. The book that caused a radical change in attitudes to cities; essential to any understanding of city growth.

Jane Jacobs *The Economy of Cities* Random House, New York, 1969

Robert Venturi *Complexity and Contradiction in Architecture* W. H. Allen, London, 1968. Museum of Modern Art, New York, 1966. The first steps to a modern architectural theory beyond functionalism.

John Summerson *Heavenly Mansions* Cresset, London, 1949

John Kenneth Galbraith *The New Industrial State* Houghton Mifflin, Boston, 1967

Viscount Esher *York, a Study in Conservation* HMSO, London, 1968

Colin Buchanan and Partners *Bath, a Study in Conservation* HMSO, London, 1968

G. S. Burrows *Chichester, a Study in Conservation* HMSO, London, 1968

Donald Insall and Associates *Chester, a Study in Conservation* HMSO, London, 1968

Four reports to the Preservation Policy Group of the UK Ministry of Housing and Local Government explore every aspect of conservation problems, both architectural and economic, and suggest a variety of strategies and remedies for environmental improvement.

Acknowledgements

Edmund Happold, a partner in the firm Ove Arup and Partners, Engineers, of London, analysed the bridge at the author's request and provided the text for Appendix 2, including the basic diagram on page 121.

Technical information on Tower Bridge has been culled from the proceedings of the Institution of Civil Engineers, 10 November 1896, *The Tower Bridge: Superstructure* by George Edward Wilson Cruttwell, and the lecture given at Carpenters' Hall, London, by Sir John Wolfe Barry in 1893.

The drawings from these publications are reproduced by courtesy of the Librarians of the respective institutes.

The drawings on pages 26, 27, 28 and 29 are from the 6 volume publication *Le Nouvel Opéra de Paris, Tome I* by J. L. Charles Garnier reproduced by courtesy of the Librarian of the Royal Institute of British Architects.

The aerial views of Tower Bridge on pages 30, 90, 114 are by Aerofilms Ltd.

The engraving on page 32 is by C. C. Schramm, Leipzig 1735, the Anglesey Abbey Loan, Fitzwilliam Museum, Cambridge.

The architectural working drawings of Tower Bridge on pages 41, 42, 43, 44, 45 and 120 are reproduced by courtesy of the City Engineer, Corporation of London.

The photograph of St Katharine's Docks redevelopment on page 47 is by Sydney W. Newbery, courtesy Taylor Woodrow.

Photographs on pages 64, 65, 116, 117 and 118 of the Tower Bridge engines are by Jean-Louis Bloch-Laine.

Drawings of Pennsylvania Station are by courtesy of the Librarian of the Royal Institute of British Architects.

The photograph on page 84 is from the Radio Times Hulton Picture Library.

The photographs on page 86 are by courtesy of *The Times* and the Ministry of Public Buildings and Works.

Photographs on page 92 are by John Donat.

The photograph on page 93 is by Eric de Maré, © Gordon Fraser.

Photographs on pages 94 and 98 are by courtesy of the Quebec information office.

The illustration on page 99 is a collage for the *Sunday Times* by Crosby/Fletcher/Forbes. The concept of Technocentres was developed by a group consisting of Kingsley/Manton/Palmer, Crosby/Fletcher/Forbes and Dennis Lyons for the Ministry of Technology.

The painting reproduced on page 111 is *A Miracle of St Zenobius* by Domenico Veneziano (1410-1461) Fitzwilliam Museum.

All other photographs are by the author.

CORPORATION
OF LONDON.
CAUTION.
THIS BASKET IS FOR
ORANGE PEEL. BANANA SKINS
OR SIMILAR REFUSE.
WHICH MUST NOT BE THROWN
UPON THE PUBLIC WAY.
By Order. TOWN CLERK

CONTENTS

Compiled by Tony Crawley. Edited by John Barraclough, Layout and design by Nigel I. Money. Published by GRANDREAMS LTD., Jadwin House, 205/211 Kentish Town Road, London NW5. Printed in Holland. ISBN 0 86227 044 8

THE BIG D
how it all began

A Sunday night it was. Sunday, April 2, 1978, to be exact. One of the three giant American TV networks, CBS, was finally giving one of its new series ideas a chance to make good. Five episodes only had been ordered — planned, cast, shot and made ready for the usual tussle with the all-important ratings. And, well, if it was any good, created a big enough stir, became important enough to sell soap / cars / toys / fridges / fruitjuices, better still if it became really so hot that the network could increase their usual advertising rates, chances were it could go to a series . . . a full season, say, of 24 shows later in the year.

Then, they'd take another look at it before considering ordering anymore from Lorimar Productions, the home of *The Waltons*.

Variety, the big entertainments trade paper, known as the Bible of Showbiz for the last 76 years, took a look at the new show. Its critic didn't think very much of it. 'A limited series,' he wrote, 'with a limited future.'

Well, you can't win them all. You can't always spot a potential winner in the great tele-sweepstakes, not from the first episode only.

'You never know with a television series,' said one of the show's stars. 'Either it catches on or it doesn't. It goes through a cycle.' And he knew what he was talking about. He's headlined three series in all: one hit, two flops.

'I never thought this show would go,' he adds. 'But now . . . well, it's gotten kinda hysterical!'

That was Larry Hagman.

And the show — what else in a book like this one — was *Dallas*.

Back in 1978, it was described quite simply — and as about as quietly as it began on the box — as a series 'of dramatic feuds in the land of the big rich.'

Now Larry Hagman and the rest of the stars are about as rich as the people they play. They're known in 64 countries in all four corners of the world — well, the free world. *Dallas* has not yet been bought in Russia or China.

Elsewhere, as we're all very much aware, the limited series with the limited success quotient is now the all-time champ of television series. Bigger than *Peyton Place*, it's forerunner in the adult-cum-spicey soap-opera. Bigger than *The Muppet Show*, bigger than *Kojak*, *Starsky and Hutch*, *Policewoman*, *Upstairs and Downstairs*.

Fifty million people watch *Dallas* every week in America (it sells a lot of soap). It was nearly double that figure in the recently wrapped third season, particularly on the night when Kristin came clean about gunning down J.R. Thirty million-plus watch it in Britain — and love the re-runs, or repeats, every bit as much as the Americans do.

Indeed, by the time all those viewers in 64 countries are totted up on the computer, *Dallas* is reaching an unbelieveable figure of 300,000,000 viewers . . .!

Shakespeare never had it this good!

Not even John Galsworthy with the BBC's eminently successful version of *The Forsyte Saga*, which also sold all over the world, did that well.

Television, more so in America, has an insatiable appetite for new shows, new people, new stories . . . *new, new, new*! New sells; old is a problem. The tube eats them up and spits them out. Millions upon millions of dollars are spent each year by the Hollywood studios in churning out the series — and more are axed than survive. Those that prove winners tend to go on for too long. *Hawaii Five O* lasted eleven years. *M*A*S*H* has been around for eight. . . .

What makes a winner, however, is never the quality of the programme, whether it's drama, comedy or musical. A winner is a show with clout. A lot of viewers. The more people who watch it, the

more who will see and hopefully be influenced, mesmerised by the commercials . . . and go out and buy the products. That's where the expression 'soap-opera' derives from. They started on radio in America in the '30s, and used to be sponsored by the soap companies.

Dallas sells a lot of soap . . . and just about every other product or device of 'necessity' needed or used, by 20th century families, from banking to insurance.

Just why *Dallas* is such a hit opens the kind of debate that could last a month. Or more. There is no one reason for its impact, just as there is no one star. (Sorry about that, Larry). *Dallas* is a heady mixture of variables.

For Americans, it's the closest thing they've ever had to adult TV-drama where talk of sex and love and affairs, oh yes and don't let's forget money, has been swiped from

where the satirical-soaps first led the way to such 'frankness' in *Mary Hartman* and *Soap*, itself.

For foreign viewers, it's the old thrill of seeing how the other half live, rich, venal Americans, up to their shoulders in oil revenue — and having to take their lumps for their lifestyle. They're all greenbacks and very little class.

Except, the *Dallas* team insist the show has nothing to do with capitalism, big oil, rich v. poor, the abuse of power or any social issues at all. (They may be right; there's very little sign, for instance, of the large Vietnamese population of Dallas in the show). It's just about emotions, say the production team. And as everything in Texas is always said to be larger, bigger, huger, than life, so is Texas emotion.

Pretty downright miserable too when you come right down to it. J.R. is about the only member of the cast to be found smiling . . . and then usually because he's metaphorically stabbed yet another partner, lover, brother, or wife in the back.

'*Dallas* makes no demands on the system,' says its creator, David Jacobs. He's definitely right there! But let's be right about him. This is *their* David Jacobs, all-American, balding and described as being 'cherubic' — not our David Jacobs.

We don't get to hear that much about J.R.'s D.J., in the million column inches the papers have devoted to the series stars, but this David Jacobs is the fella who dreamed up the Ewings and all that they've done to each other — and to themselves.

Abrasive folk, aren't they? Nothing cosy and comfy about them. Jock and Miss Ellie, JR and Sue Ellen are far removed from Mr. and Mrs. Cunningham in *Happy Days*.

The Dallasers are rather more true to life, over dramatic certainly, but almost human and believeable.

They're also just about the most despicable American family since Mario Puzo invented the Corleones in *The Godfather*. They at least had no option. They were born into the Mafia. The Ewings chose their path in life.

Jacobs was well-suited to his job as story editor of *Family* (which only ever showed up a few times, very late at night on Thames TV). He had a thing about investigating familial life. He was, for instance, most impressed by Ingmar Bergman's Swedish TV mini-series, *Scenes From A Marriage* — a mite *too* strong and true for American audiences. Jacobs wanted to do something similar and was working out some ideas when a CBS telexecutive suggested he move up country a bit, up the social ladder.

'Try something rich,' was the key expression.

Rich in America today, as in Saudi Arabia, means oil. And so, without ever going to Texas to research the place (a fact which most real Dallas citizens moan about, saying he's twisting the truth), Jacobs created the Ewings.

In fact, what he actually did first was create Pamela Barnes, 'this terribly good-looking, semi-trashy lady,' marrying into such a family. J.R. hardly got a smile in, at first. None of the Ewings did. Jacob's first idea was to follow young Pam's faltering steps into a rich, well-healed family nest, being greatly looked down upon and slowly, surely, winning their love and respect.

It was only when filling in the pieces — the background, the people owning and working the ranch — that things got out of hand — sensationally so. 'Then, I had to write a family,' said Jacobs. 'Before I had even got to a script, we had complicated things too much. We had created a ranch hand who brought her to the barbecue where she met Bobby. . . . . We had decided that the family's father was once partners with her father . . . and so on. There were soon just too many people in it to concentrate solely on her.'

And so it came to pass — and there is something distinctly Biblical as well as Shakespearean in this Ewing brood: Cain and Abel v. Romeo and Juliet — that Bobby took his new young bride home on April 2, 1978. The Ewings hit the roof of Southfork . . . and let battle commence.

Jock went mad because Pam was 'Digger' Barnes' daughter, and 'Digger' hated his guts, and indeed vice-versa. J.R. went mad, smiling all the while, because Bobby wanted back into the business and could usurp J.R.'s growing power. Digger went mad . . . well, he usually was mad with booze. And his son, Cliff Barnes, went mad. And Sue Ellen, and Lucy and Miss Ellie, they didn't look none too pleased either.

The show started just as quietly in Britain. Oh, not *another* all-American family . . .! British viewers preferred *Soap*. At first. Then, like all good drama — a serial like *The Forsyte Saga*, or a series of separate stories, welded into a single skein like *Dallas* — the emotions took hold. Characters became loved (Pam), hated (J.R.), sympathised about (Sue Ellen and Bobby), or identified with (Miss Ellie and Lucy). While it is undoubtedly true that J.R. took the series over — it could be re-named *J.R.* anytime, and in some conversations among fans, it is already — he has never been able to sink the family as he aims to. He's certainly the strongest element of the Ewing unit: a two-timing husband, businessman, cad, a thoroughly loathsome toad. Yet the more he connives against Bobby, Cliff and Ray, the more we want to see them hit back. The more he makes Sue Ellen's life an unremitting misery, the more we want to see her grab some happiness . . . whoever *he* might be!

Despite J.R.'s fame, or indeed infamy — all the stronger since he was human enough to get shot — the entire cast remains vital to what *Peyton Place* used to call 'the continuing story'.

If Lucy fades into the background

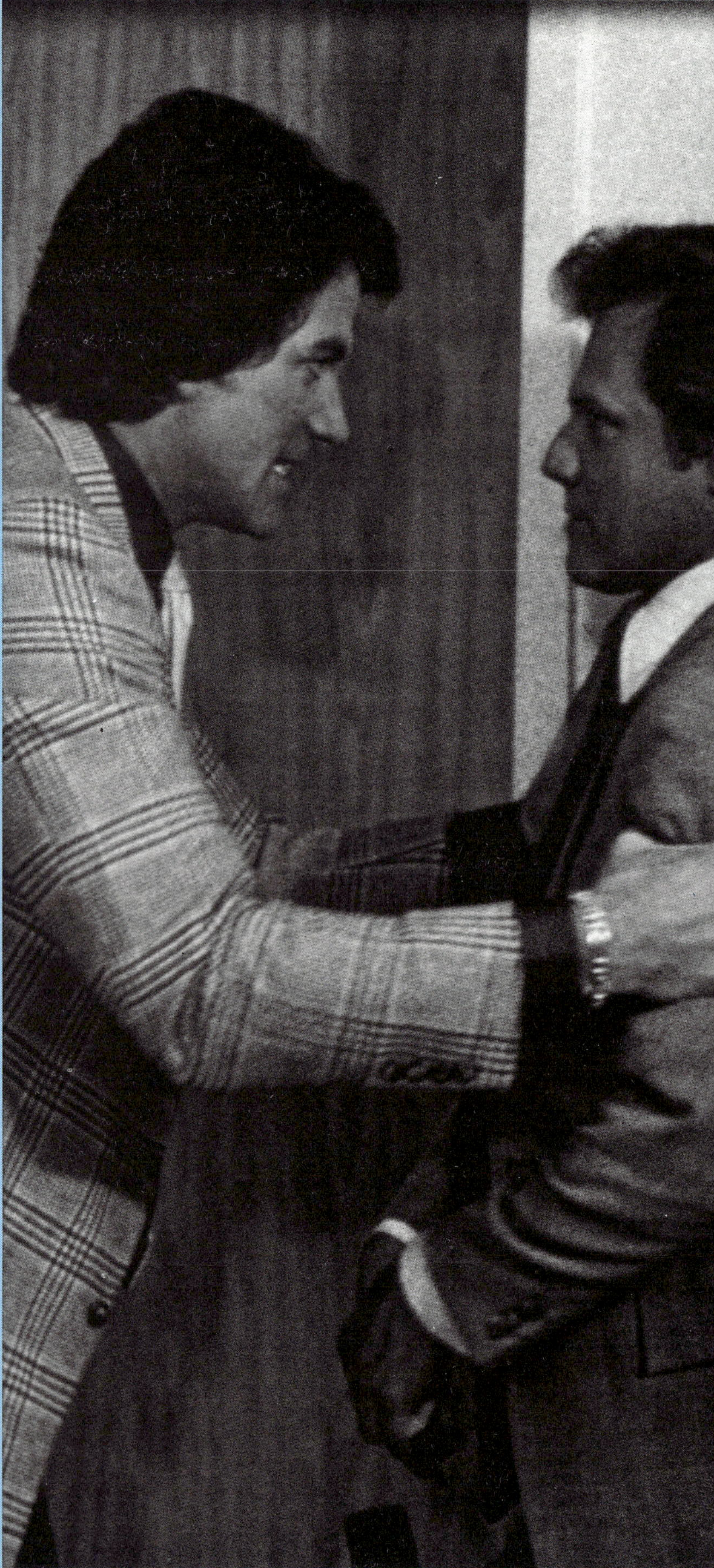

for a chapter or two, she's soon back — as a drug-addict, or up to nymphettish love games with the randy young Texans.

If Pam seems to be resting too long after yet another miscarriage (two only; it just seems more), she is suddenly starring in an episode fraught with the hereditary dangers of the disease that killed her father — except, of course, he wasn't her real father, was he?

If Bobby has been just too sweet and Sea Scout-like for months on end, he's finally turned the corner, come into his own as temporary President of Ewing Oil, churning into something of a J.R. Jnr.

If Sue Ellen gets too boring on the bottle, Cliff Barnes too neurotic in swearing to bring J.R. down, they too have sudden new departures in their characters. Alone, or as once happened, suddenly romantically entwined together.

Not even Miss Ellie, the queen motherly head of the family is without her special chapters — finding a long lost brother, or the moving account of her mastectomy fears. And Big Jock got shot once (oh yes he did!) and blurted out the facts of his previous marriage. He's also been arrested for murder . . . *and* revealed that Ray Krebbs is his illegitimate son.

Everyone gets a chance to shine on *Dallas*.

That they shine so well when given tightly scripted opportunism, is due to super casting which mixes veterans and newcomers alike. Good actors all, they've been learning from, and growing with each other since Episode One. A taut union, close, professional, no temperament as each realises the value of the other's import and input to the best series in town.

Or towns. For *Dallas* is shot both in Hollywood's MGM studios and on Texas locations in Dallas itself. Another good move. *Peyton Place* was fake, built up on the back lot of 20th Century Fox.

Southfork Ranch is really there, right enough. It's owned by a Joe Rand Duncan, so used to tourist gawkers by now, he sells them his land at $25 a turf. They buy it too!

Larry Hagman is the only true Texan in the cast. He based his J.R. city oil-slicker on oil men he met

when living there. But there are many Dallas folk who don't take kindly to Larry's interpretation of them, or the shows! They call it an insult to their town's image.

How do the stars feel about it?

Such complaints hardly phaze David Jacobs — nor Larry Hagman. 'I don't know Texas,' admits Jacobs. 'I was just working off the connections, and Dallas sounded like pure Texas. I wrote the first draft off the top of my head. I was writing for the image and not really about the place.'

'The show,' says Larry, 'is exactly what it's designed to be — entertainment. That's all. If you ever tried to put what Dallas is really all about on television — they wouldn't let you run it. You would *not* believe the level of intrigue and family feuding that goes on down there!'

'We're all having a lot of fun from it,' chips in Linda Gray. She sounds if she's speaking for the rest of us. 'I hope the show goes on forever,' she says. 'I hope the pace remains just the way it is — not any faster or slower. Right now, it's just right.'

'Honey,' drawls Charlene Tilton, 'you can say what you like, call it anything you want. We're No. 1!'

But what none of them can say, or explain, is just how the Ewings, the richest family in all of Dallas, still all . . . *live in the same house!*

THE SHOOTING OF J.R.

It's uncanny! Unbelieveable! Incomprehensible! And downright frightening! But for far too many millions of people in the world, the most important news event of the turbulent 1980 was not the Polish revolution . . . the hostages in Iran . . . the catastrophic earthquakes and volcanoes . . . the Iran-Iraqui war . . . the American presidential elections . . . or the ever-increasing unemployment figures in Great Britain.

In fact, the No. 1 topic, all the way from Philadelphia to Hong Kong, from Newcastle to Johannesburg, wasn't anything *real* at all.

It happened in America on March 21 last year and was the simulated shooting of a rapacious Texas oil baron at the hand of his low-life mistress, his wife's sister, in a popular American television series . . .

'I've certainly never heard of anything like it before,' comments Linda Gray. 'I've been talking to some people here in Hollywood who have been around the television business for *years*, and they tell me they've never seen anything like it, either,' adds Linda. 'All the newspaper and magazine articles, all the media coverage, people gambling in Las Vegas and London. . . . And we hear they actually showed the shooting on the BBC News in Britain . . . I mean it's . . . *incredible!*'

The shooting — and the long awaited denouement, delayed by more average true-life happenings, a Hollywood actors strike — has now proved to be the single most cataclysmic tele-event in the world. Fictional, that is.

Streets had emptied on March 21, 1980, the night J.R. got a bellyfull of lead. They emptied again on November 21 when Kristin coughed . . . as brazenly as ever.

How much one might enjoy catching up with the doings of the Ewings, from time to time, this rather gigantic craze for the series was without precedent in TV history. Some commentators felt it presented a rather sick view of society in the global village.

Fifty-three countries tuned in to the shooting . . . the headline-making news of which helped sell the series to another eleven countries by the time it came back on the air again.

It had just got out of hand! Certainly out of planning.

The *Dallas* producer, Leonard Katzman, and J.R. himself, Larry Hagman, agree that it will soon be forgotten. Besides, they want to put it behind them now. There's plenty of other shocks being cooked up for the future. . . .

Lorimar doesn't expect to cause such a phenomenon again. They didn't figure on causing the first one at all. The whole notion of J.R. Ewing being shot was a postscript really.

The second year's series should have ended with the two-hour account of Jock's trial — when Big Daddy was finally let off the hook when his old foe (and the father, in fact, of the D.A. trying the case) confessed to the murder of Hutch McKinney. What's more, old 'Digger' Barnes on his deathbed proved that the late Mr. McKinney was Pam Ewing's real father.

Shock! Horror! End! See y'all again same place, same spot on your dial next September.

But no . . .

Dallas had really started rolling in that second year. And the CBS network, leading the ratings battle because of it, acted like any other network. It wasn't only content with too much of a good thing. It wanted more. Two more episodes at least before closing up shop for the season.

Now that was a mite tough. The writing team had worked towards and hit their big climax for their year. The holidays were coming . . . and they were spent.

But producer Lenny Katzman is not what Larry Hagman calls 'the smartest man in the business' for nothing. He agreed, something could be worked out. Just what, though, he had no idea.

Picture the scene, Katzman's office at the MGM Studios. He's talking with the series executive producer, Phil Capice. They kick around a few ideas for two more stories. Maybe Pam can...? Why doesn't Lucy...? Then Capice speaks up for all *Dallas* fans and J.R. foes. 'Let's,' says Phil, '...let's have J.R. get his.'

Eureka!

'We didn't know who shot him,' explains Lenny Katzman. 'We said, "The hell with that. Let's shoot him and figure out who did it later." Then, we started eliminating and eliminating until we found the person we wanted.'

Larry Hagman was not overly taken with the shooting idea. It lacked, he thought, imagination. Realising that at least two, if not four, fictional characters are shot every night of the week, on all three American networks, not forgetting the hundreds of local stations running old shows, he was right, of course.

Larry suggested J.R. should walk into the Ewing Oil elevator — and fall down 15 floors. No lift!

Hmm? Too imaginative, perhaps.

Still in their huddle, Katzman and Capice began tying in J.R.'s demise (or sudden ill-health, at least) with a suicide attempt by Sue Ellen. . . . She fixes herself the ultimate nightcap, goes off to kiss her baby son goodbye. Enter J.R., drunk, in need of a hair of the dog, spies Sue Ellen's glass of hot (barbiturate) toddy, and downs it in one go. Sue Ellen sees all, does nothing, says nothing, returns to baby John, and rocks his cot. Dissolve. Shock. Horror. End.

'No,' said the huddled producers. Imaginative, yes. But not as much fun as creating a whole bunch of whodunnit suspects — and they had enough of those on file. Six at least, although Mary Crosby, the eventual sniper as Kristin, counted as many as 18 from the previous story skeins.

Did they really want to get rid of him ?

When J.R. got shot, viewers didn't know if he was dead or alive. Larry Hagman's own scenario for the cliff-hanger, falling 15 storeys down an open lift-shaft, seemed to indicate he preferred J.R. to die. To literally drop out of Dallas.

And for a while during that long, hot, drawn out summer of actors striking and galloping inflation, and all the other financial and social ills which struck Hollywood as heavily as, say, Manchester, there seemed a distinct possibility that Larry Hagman would leave the series.

Not J.R. mind you. Just good old Lar'.

Hagman says he never wanted to quit. All he was after was a fair day's wage for appearing in what had become the world's toppermost TV entertainment. The network could afford it. Dallas *made rich profits every which way, from selling ad. time on their commercial breaks, to selling the hit-show throughout the world.*

On the night Kristin confessed, commercials on Dallas *time cost $500,000 per minute. On that one night alone, the CBS network made $2,350,000 profit. In one hour!*

'I may never get another chance like this in my lifetime,'

Hagman said when explaining his salary-fight to Playboy magazine. 'If you've got a chance to make it — make it! Frankly, I don't think anyone *is worth this kind of money. I think it's ridiculous except that's the way it is. It may be out of proportion, but I'd be a fool not to take advantage of it.*

'Everybody's got rises,' adds Larry Hagman, 'that's the most important thing. Me? Let's say they pay me what I think I'm worth!'

Fine, but that doesn't answer the nagging question behind all this financial wheeler-dealering. Would Leonard Katzman and Lorimar Productions have dumped Hagman and found another J.R.?

'Well, of course they would,' booms Larry. 'Believe me, if I hadn't come back, they would have found someone else. Dallas *doesn't* need *me. It's hot! It's got the roll!'*

And in point of historic fact, the third year of Dallas *did roll — without Larry Hagman. He didn't show for the first two episodes. That body of J.R., bound up in bandages like* The Invisible Man, *being rolled away on an ambulance gurney, being operated on in hospital — that wasn't Larry Hagman at all. That was good old Lar's double, a gent named Ace Moore.*

Indeed, while Hagman continued haggling about money, and J.R. was recovering in the Dallas Hospital and would soon be required to speak again, glower again, be seen again (hardly smiling this time), the producers were busily engaged in the job of finding another actor should Hagman not return.

If Hagman hadn't won his deal, and had kept his promise to quit, the new J.R. would have been Robert Culp, the star of the comedy thriller series, I Spy *in the mid-60s, plus films like* Bob and Carol and Ted and Alice.

There was even a scripted explanation all ready typed to cover J.R.'s sudden change of face. A bullet had struck him right in the everlasting smile. He would require plastic surgery and when the bandages came off, no longer look like he did in previous programmes.

Would we have accepted a new J.R.? of course we would.

Even Larry Hagman appreciates that fact of life. Dallas, *as he says, is still a show without a star. It's a team of stars, an ensemble casting coup.*

Actors have quit the series before now, or been unable to continue roles due to other commitments. Ted Shackelford took over Gary Ewing's role from David Ackroyd. Keenan Wynn followed David Wayne into 'Digger' Barnes' shoes.

Even Mary Crosby wasn't the original Kristin — that was . . . well, no, we're not giving away all the answers to our quiz here.

BIG JOCK
the Duke of Dallas

JIM DAVIS is Jock Ewing — John Ewing I — the oil and cattle baron of Southfork Ranch, the steel in the family's spine; gruff, grim, tough as old hard-tack, he's clawed his way to the top — and sure plans to stay there.

Seven years ago when Hollywood decided — as telexecutives often do — to make a TV series based on a hit movie, they hit a snare. The film they'd chosen was The Cowboys. *The star of which would hardly be interested in working around the clock for television. No siree, not John Wayne.*

Who, then, could replace such a monument like Big John...?

The producers really didn't have to think twice about that. They picked up the phone, dialled Northridge, California, and talked to... big Jim Davis.

Jim, who used to be billed as James back in the '40s (doesn't quite ring true, does it?) has made more Western movies than any other kind. He's ridden, shot and fought with just about every cowpoke star on the range. From The Duke to Lee Marvin. From 'Wild' Bill Elliott to Rod Cameron. Why, he even turned up once in Alias Jesse James *in 1959 with the wildest, roughest, rooting-tootingest cowboy of 'em all. Bob Hope!*

Big Jim has ridden through the entire spectrum of horse-operas the good, the bad and the ugly, the straight, psychological and satiric, the million-dollar epics and the el cheapo featurettes. He's as much home on the range in A or B Westerns. And for why? Because he looks the part. Larry Hagman was born in cowboy country — Texas — not Jim. He arrived in Missouri 66 years ago, but he's the one Dallas star who looks as if he was born in the saddle. At 6ft 3ins he's made for cowboy boots. Looks better still on a horse. Like all true Western heroes, he's tall — mighty tall — in the saddle.

He was, therefore, also first choice for the oil millionaire and cattle baron Jock Ewing when Dallas *came into being. Jim had all the right stuff for the part. Once again, he* looked *exactly how a Jock Ewing would look. That very American kind of rough diamond, up from no place in particular to the very top of the Texan heap, running his own dukedom, asssisted by his cunning, guile — and guts.*

He's made Ewing Oil what it is. He's made the Ewing clan what it is, too. And all the family, his sons or their womenfolk, suffer from his bad traits, as well as (occasionally) excelling in his good points. J.R., of course, is as much a maverick as Jock is... or was. Only thing that's different about their business ethics is the era they live in. Jock settled most of his arguments with a fist or, so it's been said, a gun. J.R. resorts to city-slicker blackmail and other abused powers of his lofty position in Dallas society... like all but owning the police force!

But really, whatever ole J.R. gets up to today — or tomorrow — one look at ole Jock's face tells you, he's done it all before. And probably worse. Fact is, he'd like to be out there still sticking it to them now... except for that dicky heart, he would be. And there are those in Dallas who'd prefer to deal with treacherous J.R. than Jock when he gets riled...

Jim Davis, in fact, is one of the few members of the cast to have had anything to do with the oil industry. Larry Hagman, during his on-off acting days, actually made oil pipe springs for a living ('and by hand, lemme tell ya!') but Jim was closely involved with the intricacies of the business before going out and selling the finished stuff as a top salesman for a leading oil concern. That followed his year as a rigger with a travelling circus tent-show, when straight out of college in Missouri.

It was the oil biz, which brought Jim into show biz. He was promoted to Los Angeles, and soon enough was mixing with the ritzy pre-war movie fraternity. Well, no, he didn't socialise with them too much. He still doesn't. He stood back from it all, and examined them and began to hanker after their lifestyle.

Took his time, though, did Jim. He never moves hastily. Having once checked into all the ins and outs of the oil industry before going to work for it, he applied much the same techniques to investigating the acting game. He worked hard at it, too, while pretending all the time not to be interested in acting at all.

He signed for some acting lessons. He got himself back into his college-boy shape at a gymnasium. Most vital, of all, he signed with a reputable agent.

So, he was all ready to go — but on his terms. (He's very much like Jock Ewing in this respect.) When film producer Pandro Berman offered him an MGM studio contract something most raw actors would have sold their grandmothers' graves for, Jim simply shook his head. Nope! 'Hell,' he told Berman, 'I make more money in the oil business.'

Berman was impressed! He'd never been turned down before; he was the guy that did all the rejecting... He arranged a screen test for Jim and another possible newcomer to MGM's celebrated list of 'more stars than there are in heaven' — swimmer Esther Williams. After the test, they both got offered parts. Jim took a dekko at his new deal, noticed the new, much hiked up money. This time,

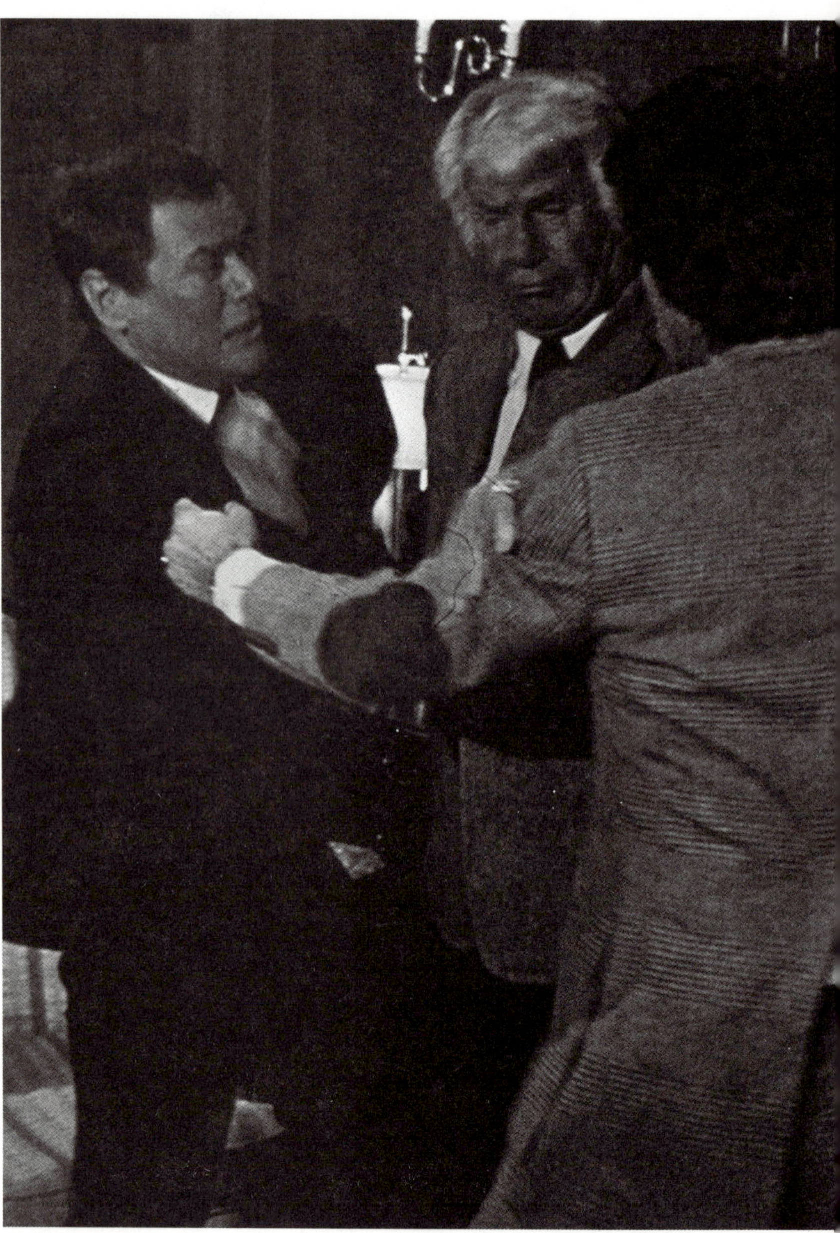

he said: Sure. (Now, years later he's back at the Metro studios, shooting Dallas*).*

He started in the movie equivalent of the back row in the chorus. With one-liner roles (if they had anything to say, at all). He moved up to leading roles in some crime shorts, and then co-starred with Ann Southern in her Maisie *series of comedies.*

Like so many others in various occupations, Jim Davis was just getting rolling when the Japanese invaded Pearl Harbour. He rushed into the war with what remained of the U.S. Navy. When he returned to MGM later, he co-starred with baby-faced Van Johnson in Romance of Rosie Ridge *— and then asked for his release from his contract with Leo the Lion. He wanted to freelance, doing his own thing, finding parts as they fell.*

He got on very well indeed. The life of a character actor is often far more remunerative than that of a star. Jim Davis was rarely out of the saddle. The Fabulous Texan, Red Stallion in the Rockies, California Passage, The Iron Mistress, Last Stagecoach, West.

He took a respite from the Westerns by playing a naval officer in love with his namesake Bette Davis, in Winter Meeting *(1948)... and that, perhaps, was his big spot until becoming Jock Ewing.*

Not that he has been retired inbetween. Far from it. Jim Davis has made more than 150 movies, from one-liner parts to leading roles as either heavy or hero: Cavalry Scout, The Fighting 7th, The Last Command, Timberjack, The Maverick Queen, Fort Utah, Rio Lobo, Big Jake, The Honkers, Bad Company, Monte Walsh. *As if that wasn't enough for one career, he's also starred in as many as 300 TV shows, toplining series like* Story of the Century, Rescue 8, Rivermen *and* The Cowboys... *plus tele-movies galore,* The Trackers, Deliver Us From Evil, The Smokeaters, Satan's Triangle, Stone, Just A Little Inconvenience.

In one of his most recent big screen releases, the science fiction thriller, The Day Time Ended, *big Jim, the patriarch of Southfork, played the husband of Dorothy Malone, the queen of that other big American TV soap-opera triumph,* Peyton Place...!

In all, Jim has certainly made more movie and TV shows than the rest of the Dallas *cast put together — with the possible exception of his old enemy in the show, Keenan Wynn, alias 'Digger' Barnes. Yet, Jim Davis still finds time for the golf he loves, and the woman he adores — his wife, Blanche.*

'Oh sure,' he grins, 'I really am Jock Ewing... without the money.' With his kind of track record, he must be awfully close, though.

DEADLY KRISTIN
she done him wrong!

MARY CROSBY, Bing's only daughter, is Kristin Shepard, Sue Ellen's kid sister, a tough babe to cross, as brother-in-law J.R. found out late one night in his office. And as we all know now . . . at last!

'Of course, shedunnit,' screamed Time magazine evolving yet another new word for the slanguage dictionaries. 'The co-ed vamp with a mean streak as deep as her cleavage,' continued Richard Corliss' expert description of the guilty party. 'The pedler of her own educated flesh. The Mata Hari of Ewing Oil. The counterspy for the nefarious lawyer Alan Beam. The scheming sister of Mrs. J. R. Ewing. The seducer of the ultimate seducer, Mr. J. R. Ewing, and the self-proclaimed carrier of his child. What apter justice? The person who fired the shots heard round the world was the female J.R., Kristin Shepard.

Well, of course, it was. Was there really any doubt . . .?

Mary Crosby kept the entertainment world's biggest secret all the time she was in London shooting her *Dick Turpin* film with Richard O'Sullivan.

'That was easy,' she grins. 'Because I didn't know. None of us knew whodunnit until we shot the episode that told all.'

There was something of a clue given out, and largely unheeded, when Lorimar, the company making *Dallas*, announced that Mary would be leaving the series after the fifth episode of the third series. She kept a straight face about it. 'They need new people all the time,' was her only comment. And by then she knew. About forty people at Lorimar knew. They still kept quiet though.

Mary was offered $10,000 by one avid fan for the information. In Britain, Larry Hagman was offered much more, £100,000 if he'd tell. And he couldn't — then — even if he'd wanted to.

Keeping The Big Secret was vital. There had been such a huge wait for the unmasking of the sniper. The *Dallas* stars, already in shock at the kind of impact their series was making around the world, wondered just how much longer their public would wait. Would they *bother* to watch *Dallas* again after a nine months lay-off?

Would they not!

The all-important episode, transmitted in America and Britain on the same weekend in November, 1980, sent the ratings through the roof. In America, it won the biggest-ever audience in the history of U.S. television.

Mary Crosby's shining hour, then. A long way from warbling with her Dad, the late Bing Crosby, on his oh-so-cosy Christmas TV family get-togethers.

She got her wish. Of the 18 or more people she reckoned could have shot J.R., she ended up with the smoking gun — pinched, naturally, from Sue Ellen. And later

planted back in J.R.'s closet to further incriminate his poor wife, by then unconscious in the airport parking lot, after being slipped a mickey finn by the vengeful Kristin!

As Hollywood columnist Jim Bacon wrote about Mary, before she entered the Southfork saga: 'She's going to be dynamite. She has the beauty of a young Elizabeth Taylor, and the drive of a Bette Davis. How can you beat a combination like that?'

Mary is certainly the most successful of Bing Crosby's seven children (his only daughter, from his second marriage to actress Kathryn Grant). She was brought up in the fairly pampered way most movie stars' kids are, but Mary exerted her fiery independence early on. She was 13, when volunteering for an exchange student programme, and went off to study in Mexico, swopping Bing Crosby's luxury living for room and board with a poor Mexican family, helping with all the chores for their seven kids.

She never really lived off her family name until she felt good and ready to succeed with it. After studies at her mother's alma mater, the University of Texas at Austin, she auditioned for the prestigious American Conservatory Theatre in San Francisco, and won a place in their two year training programme. She was so unassuming, no one even thought of asking if she was Bing's daughter. 'She just didn't act like any big star's kid,' says a fellow student. 'She just did her thing, from carrying a spear in *Julius Caesar* to tackling the lead in a Gorky play, just like any other good student.'

She picked more true stage experience in the vacations, acting with her mother in summer stock productions of *Sabrina Fair, The Prime of Miss Jean Brodie*, in America — and taking *The Heiress* further afield to Scotland, while Bing was on the golf courses.

It was only after Bing died — on another course in Spain, October 14, 1977 — that Mary Crosby dared test her wings — and fly solo. She had immediate success from 1978 onwards. She won two tele-movies, *With This Ring* and *Guide For The Married Woman*. She played a mute rape victim in *Starsky and Hutch*, a frightened child in *Pearl*, and a college girl in *Brothers and Sisters* . . . not her favourite show.

Everything was going well for her. While with the A.C.T. in San Francisco, she had met, fallen in love and lived with her husband today, Ed Lottimar, a young composer and music publisher. They were wed in November 1978, just as *Dallas* finally began to hit its stride in America.

Kristin Shepard turned up twice in that first series — trying to steal Bobby away from Pam in one story. She was then played by Colleen Camp. Mary took over the role, more meatier and manipulative and with J.R. as *her* target, in late 1979. 'The roles I've taken on since my father's death might not have thrilled him, but I know he'd be proud of my success as an actress,' says Mary. 'He was a good father. He was also extremely conservative. He publicly said — and I wish he hadn't — that he would disown a daughter of his that lived with a man before marriage.'

Mary did just that — a move that annoyed her mother. Everything seems smoothed out now that Mary and Ed are married, a fine home in Malibu . . . and there's a new superstar in the Crosby family.

THE EWING FAMILY ALBUM

John Ross Ewing, Snr.

Eleanor Ewing

John Ross Ewing, Jnr.

Sue Ellen Ewing

Robert Ewing

Pamela Ewing

Lucy Ewing Cooper

BOBBY

Big Brother is watching him.

PATRICK DUFFY is Bobby Ewing, Jock's youngest sprout off the Ewing tree, the conscience of the tribe, the doting husband of Pam, and something of an idealistic innocent among the family's power struggles, aghast at big brother's business methods and their father's approval of them.

The news that Ray Krebbs is really another of Jock's offspring, really made one wonder if Bobby is one at all. He is, after all, curiously misplaced in the Southfork menagerie. The surprise liberal in a family of such arch-conservatives. The knight in shining armour, tilting at windmills and forever being toppled into cow flaps by... well, who else but big brother!

Bobby's wife, Pam, twice got pregnant then lost the babies. J.R.'s. fault! Bobby keeps getting uptight at the way the family combine is run. J.R.'s fault! Bobby is eternally coming or going, either charging out of Southfork with his wife in tow — again, J.R.'s fault! — or coming back home with a lost sheep or two, like Gary and Val. And what drove them away in the first place. You're right in one. J.R.'s fault!

Bobby, it was, who started the series causing the kind of screaming match we've come to expect, by bringing home his new wife. The Ewings have never really trusted Pam (J.R.'s fault! He said she was a spy for Cliff Barnes). To tell the truth, the Ewings were none too sure about Bobby for a good while after that, either.

Until, that is J.R. was flattened by Kristin (and that was definitely J.R.'s fault!). Then Bobby finally got the chance he's been moaning for all over the place for the last few years — to take control of Ewing Oil. His way.

From the third year on of Dallas, therefore, we began to see a radical change in ole Bob. 'Less pure as he comes more powerful,' is how producer Leonard Katzman phrased it. In short: St. Bobby's halo started to slip. Well you know what they say about absolute power — it corrupts absolutely. Look what it did to J.R.

And shot or not, big-shot J.R. is still watching over Bobby. It's his business, the kid is running. It's J.R. who wants it

back. All of it. And it's J.R. who will move mountains to do just that, you can bet your bottom dollar on it. 'I'm really very grateful that the whole series has gone the way it has,' says Pat Duffy. 'I'm just beginning to get back down to earth from all of it. Now that we've been around for awhile, I'm getting used to it. For the first time, I feel I've the hang of what I'm doing. It's a good feeling.'

Sure looks that way. The jokes about Bobby are beginning to pall. J.R. is the new fall guy.

Like some others of the cast, Patrick Duffy almost didn't join the Dallas series. He had less than a week to make up his mind. That's the few days between the sudden axing of his first TV series, the ill-fated Man From Atlantis, and the first day of production of Dallas on location in Texas.

That wasn't much time and Pat had been rushed all the way through Atlantis and didn't like it. It was his first taste of the goal of many new actors — his own series, his first brush with fame... and he never had time to enjoy it. Scripts, as per usual in Tellyland, were rushed, the series kept having its time-slot switched. Changes were always being made at the last second. Is it a kiddy show? Is it adult science fiction? Nobody seemed to know, week to week. The star himself didn't know if he was coming or going.

Having stuck that for a few months, he was obviously none too excited at the prospect of immediately leapfrogging into another series. The casting impressed him, though — Barbara Bel Geddes' name worked like magic. The story outlines, too, seemed to make sense. Dallas had some power and guts, some flesh and blood, three-dimensional characters — not soggy cardboard like Mark Harris, the underwater amphibian of the Atlantis show.

He said yes, of course. His career changed overnight. He's now a big wheel, with his own production company, various projects on the boil to keep him busy during the long summer lay-offs between series-making... like the tele-movie, Enola Gay, about the crew of the USAF plane that dropped the first Atom bomb on Hiroshima.

Pat Duffy hails from a small Montana town called Townsend — from end to end it has room for just about 600 people. When he was 12, his family moved to Seattle, Washington, and being a good schoolboy athlete, he had dreams of becoming a top sports pro. His school's drama teacher had other ideas. He persuaded Pat to audition for the Professional Actors' Training Programme at Washington University. More than 1200 would-be thespians were seen for a dozen vacancies in the four year programmes. Duffy was one of them. So far so good...

'The training encompassed everything from medieval works to modern theatre, with a heavy emphasis on Shakespeare,' explains Patrick. 'We had some of the finest instructors possible. Mime teachers from France. Gymnasts from the Olympics. Even jugglers from Barnum and Bailey's circus!'

The young Duffy worked at acting round the clock. So much so he ruptured both vocal chords. A specialist offered him two grim options. Surgery, with no success guaranteed. Or an undetermined period of silence, rigidly enforced.

Pat chose silence. He got his voice back and then in the kind of neat plot that even J.R. would appreciate, he suggested the position of 'actor in residence' at Washington State University — and filled the post himself. The work entailed acting as interpreter for visiting ballet, opera and orchestra companies, with time off to teach movement and mime on the side.

The job was the best stroke Patrick Duffy pulled in his life. Because that's how he met his pretty wife, Carlyn — a ballerina with the First Chamber Dance Company of New York. She urged him to quit Washington and try acting in New York's busy theatreland. He wasn't too successful in the Big Apple. Just the one decent off-

Broadway play, Natural Affection. *But top agent Joan Scott caught him in it, signed him up and told him: Go West, young man.*

Once installed in Hollywood, he found himself a couple of tele-movie quickies, The Stranger Who Looks Like Me *and* Hurricane. *By 1975, work was thin on the ground, he joined San Diego's Old Globe company to keep his acting muscles in trim... he was back with Shakespeare.*

He returned to television in the CBS production of The Last of Mrs. Lincoln. *The next call was about this Atlantean who could swim underwater for days but not walk around for too long on earth: Mark Harris,* The Man From Atlantis! *And before Mark's funeral was over, he'd become Bobby Ewing...*

Patrick Duffy — born, by the way, or did you guess, on St. Patrick's Day, March 17 — lives very quietly, far from the fuss and brouhaha of the Hollywood party circuits, in Southern California. He has a large house which he and Carlyn are renovating themselves. 'Well,' Pat grins, you know that sheepish grin, 'with a little help from our sons, Padraic and Conor.'

The Duffys are both Buddhists these days, and probably the keenest of the Dallas *star families on physical fitness. They tend to keep themselves to themselves. If they go into Los Angeles for an evening out, it's more likely to be to catch a visiting top ballet troupe, symphony orchestra or British stage company than for any ritzy movie premiere.*

Patrick, however, has been coming out of his shell as much as Bobby, of late. Ironically, when the third series of Dallas *was held up by the Hollywood actors' strike, Pat was one of the leading strike activists. He carried banners and made speeches along with his friends, Ed Asner and Daryl Anderson (Lou and Animal from the* Lou Grant *series).*

None of them was particularly delighted at the terms which ended the strike. Backed by Asner, both Pat and Daryl have since been elected to the board of directors of the Screen Actors' Guild — the Hollywood film and TV actors' union.

J.R. had better watch his step. Patrick Duffy is no longer the Boy Sea Scout Joke. He's an unshakable new power. On and off the set.

NAUGHTY LUCY

the spoilt grandchild

CHARLENE TILTON is Lucy Ewing, daughter of the exiled Gary and Valene, niece of J.R. and Bobby, grand-daughter of Miss Ellie and Jock . . . and trouble to one and all. Now that she's wed, do you really think that's all going to change?

Hollywood — well, Tellywood, then — has a big thing about big blondes. Angie Dickinson . . . Farrah Fawcett . . . Suzanne Sommers . . . Susan Anton . . . Loni Anderson. . . . Now Charlene Tilton is all the rage.

She's probably the naughtiest blonde in Hollywood history. She's certainly the smallest blonde in Hollywood since the heyday of Shirley Temple.

Terry Wogan probably made her even more famous than *Dallas* did when dubbing her The Poison Dwarf. Cruel, but true. About Lucy Ewing that is, not Charlene Tilton. Lucy, after all, is probably more capable of more downright evil than even Uncle J.R., . . . if (like him) she doesn't get her way.

Remember the day she tried to get out of school by saying one of the staff has assaulted her? Or how about the birthday party she left in a huff, just ran off, hitched a ride . . . and found herself held hostage by a nutty thief . . .? And her experimenting with drugs . . .?

Well, yes, such ventures could well explain why she's been spoilt rotten by Miss Ellie and the rest.

A veritable Lolita of the Texas ranges, Lucy Ewing is a rich creation (not fully mined as yet) by the *Dallas* writing team — and, of course, by Charlene Tilton, tilting up to just about 5ft on the tape measure.

Charlene is the youngest of the star cast — as the daughter of divorced parents, Gary and Valene Ewing, currently reunited, alive and well and living (surrounded by gossip) in *Knots Landing*.

They were kicked out of Southfork by J.R. (Who else?). Not that he admitted as much to young Lucy. His version was that they abandoned her. That Gary left Dallas in another of his drunken binges. That Val took out after him — or straight to the divorce courts.

J.R. has done his level best to get rid of Lucy, too. He just can't stand the possibility of opposition, can he? He planned to marry her off to Alan Beam (another pain in J.R.'s neck), and settle them both way off in Illinois some place. Lucy played both men along for a while. As long as it suited her, before pulling out of any such wedding plans.

She took great delight in spiking Uncle J.R.'s guns and eventually married who she wanted to — the series newest blond handsome Leigh McCloskey.

Well, maybe it's high time the boisterous Lucy settled down. If, that is, you tend to view this marriage as a settling down process at all.

'I enjoy being controversial,' says Charlene about her role. 'When Lucy came on the scene, it was the right time for a bad woman to start making an appearance on night-time TV — and the public sure loved it. Me, too. I enjoyed growing up from the wicked teenager to a mature woman.'

She was also fairly new to the business then. Still wet behind the ears, although she had been acting most of her 17 years. In an amateur way. She kicked off in high school (where she was also, almost inevitably with a figure like hers a cheerleader). She made her first film at 16 — in Walt Disney's comedy *Freaky Friday* (1976) with Jodie Foster. Charlene didn't have to travel far to get to work. Although born up the state apiece in San Diego, she had been living in Hollywood most of her life.

After acting with her high school's drama club, she worked in neighbourhood theatres in Los Angeles hoping for a break into movies, or TV. Nothing! She was working part-time in a tee-shirt shop when she met Jon Mercedes, fell for him, moved in with him. They were certainly good for each other at the time (they've since separated). He made sure she quit her job to spend more time chasing up acting work.

In the year between working on the Disney film and joining the *Dallas* cast from the first episode, she made two big movies — John Milius' *Big Wednesday* and *Sweater Girls* — and about eight tele-guest roles, warming up The Fonz and Co. in *Happy Days*, Angie Dickinson's *Police Woman*, Lindsay Wagner's *Bionic Woman* and *The Love Boat*, among others.

Since her *Dallas* fame, she's also been making good use of her hiatus time, the vacations between series shooting, by starring in tele-flicks. She appears in the re-make of Edgar Allen Poe's *Fall of the House of Usher* and in a drama called *Diary of a Teenage Hitchhiker*. Added to which are her commercials and her regular sunny appearances on the *Hollywood Squares* panel show.

A busy bird, then. No wonder she has little time in which to grow.

She's not finding it an easy matter to lose her sexy tele-image. On the other hand, she doesn't seem to be trying too hard — keeping that delightful figure well in good order by weekly gymnastics, horse-riding, water-ski-ing and the most popular pursuit along Santa Monica's Venice Beach — roller-skating.

'Well,' she has said, 'there is always a tendency to be stereotyped. People on the streets . . .' She stops, and smiles. . . . 'Well, the men anyway . . . they think of me as something of a nymphomaniac. You wouldn't believe how many propositions I get in person and through the mail.'

Oh yes, we would.

THE HUMAN OIL SLICK

~why J.R. is the hate we love to love!

He's turning 50, walks with a stick, is a trifle hard of hearing, a Texan, an Episcopalian who doesn't want to be buried 'but minced!', an 'outrageous eccentric' by self-admission, never speaking on Sundays, spending as much free time as he can muster in jacuzzi baths at home ('the family that bathes together, stays together'), leading bizarrely garbed parades along Malibu beach, going shopping at the local supermarket in a gorilla suit, collecting and wearing a mad assortment of hats from grey toppers to Indian head-dress ('no I'm *not* bald, don't have a toupee, I've just worn hats for 30 years because they look good!'), draping and hanging flags anywhere he settles, doing more for the new Western style of fashion in America, and beyond, than John Travolta's *Urban Cowboy*, and swimming a length of his small pool by tying himself to the centre of the pool with a rope and not actually moving anywhere! He used to play a straight-laced U.S.A.F. astronaut with a girl genie in a bottle, now has his latest TV wife similarly locked into a bottle (of hooch), has been married to the same woman for 27 years, has two children, a Mercedes car, a Malibu beach house, earns considerably more than the President of the United States (about $1.65 million a year) and has been described, variously, by Playboy as 'an overstuffed Iago in a stetson' and by his extremely televisual spouse, Linda Gray, as 'the biggest sex-symbol on TV since Farrah Fawcett.'

Who else could it be but... Larry Hagman!

Or, as he's better known, loved, hated, adored, impugned, admired, admonished, revered and reviled by a record-breaking 300,000,000 televiewers around the globe: John Ross Ewing, Jnr.

The abbreviations on the end will suffice. J.R.

The man we love to hate. The hate we love to love. The human oil slick. The terror of Texas. The devil of Dallas. The slimey scumbag of Southfork Ranch.

The smiler with a dirk in his smirk...

'It's true,' agrees his wife, Maj. 'He has the most awful smile! It's devilish! When he walks into a room with that certain smile on his face, everyone knows that something is up... and about to happen.

'There's always been an excitement about Larry. I suppose the reason all those women love J.R. is because he's a challenge. They all want to change him.'

'Fat chance,' snorts Larry, good ole Lar' as he refers to himself. (Like J.R., he's hardly modest). 'Why any woman in her right mind would want him is beyond me. I guess J.R. is attractive to women because they love middle-aged men. And like Kissinger said, power is an aphrodisiac... I guess it is sexy!'

Sure, but isn't he also horrid, rotten, despicable, evil, the viper in Miss Ellie's bosom, a libertine, a renegade ingrate and scapegrace... a 100% gilt-edged louse with it?

Larry looks shocked. 'No, no, far from it,' he drawls, with a look that seems to say: How can you be so wrong about this poor fella.

'He's takin' care of business, is all. Takin' care of the family. It's the old American ethic, mah friend!'

Sue Ellen, Bobby, Cliff Barnes, Alan Beam, Ray Krebbs and Vaughn Leland and all the rest of his victims might not necessarily agree with that.

He looks shocked again. 'If people get in the way, they've gotta take the lumps.'

J.R. has been dishing out the lumps — to all and sundry — for three years now. And making himself a mint. Good ole Lar' is not far behind him. He's just never had it this good. Oh, he's had fame before. Heaps of it! He was the star of that girlie-genie-in-a-bottle rubbish, I Dream of Jeannie, for five hard-slog years with Barbara Eden from 1965. That typecast him as a straight man, very straight, not a mean bone in his body, for the next few years. He co-starred with the original 'Digger' Barnes, David Wayne in The Good Life (nothing to do with the BBC series of the same name), and Hagman, the hangman of Dallas, was given pert brunette Diane Baker as a wife for 15 episodes of something equally daffy called Here We Go Again.

That's rather what he thought when, after a whole bunch of films — The Eagle Has Landed providing him with another of his frequent trips to his much-loved Britain — his agent called up with news about two new TV series in the offing at Lorimar Productions. Larry's agent felt he'd fit into either of them real well. He wasn't pushing for either. Larry could make up his own mind.

One of the pair was a situation comedy called The Waverly Wonders about a basketball team, the other was a drama slot named Dallas. He didn't feel either of them would make it beyond the pilot, or test show. But as he'd had his bellyfull of sit-coms, thank you very much, he plumped for Dallas. There was something in it that appealed to his imagination and flair for characterisation.

'There wasn't one redeeming person in it,' he explained to Time magazine. 'Even the mother was bad. I was tired of shows in which everybody was so nice and warm and cuddly to each other.'

And yet he still calls J.R. 'kinda cute!'

He made the right decision, of course. The Waverly Wonders wondered what hit them, being cancelled in very rapid order. And Dallas, though it started out sort of

quietly, is now the No. 1 television series in the world.

His fan mail is filled with some of the most amazing offers and propositions from women lusting after his middle-aged body. They send their photographs, too.

'I'm just having fun,' he told Playboy recently. 'About the time it starts to get on my nerves, it will be dying down anyway. It'll all be gone in another 30, 40 seconds.'

It took him 31 years to get to No. 1. He was born into show business — and into Texas, in fact. His mother is the musical comedy star, Mary Martin, 76 years young and still packing 'em in. His father, who died when Larry was 33, had other ideas for him — to follow him into the law.

The Hagmans lived in Texas, where Larry was born in Fort Worth on September 21, 1931. Following his parents' divorce five years later, he stayed with his mother, or rather with her mother, Mary Martin was too occupied chasing after stardom — eventually winning through in her big *stage hits of* Annie Get Your Gun, South Pacific *and* Peter Pan.

Young Larry was shoved through various private and military schools — sixteen in all. He didn't like them. But the one he really loved in Vermont, didn't rate him too highly, either — after he burned down the boy's dormitory. He was 14 at the time.

After being fired for firing the dorms, Larry went back

to live with his father — in Weatherford, Texas. Ben Hagman worked hand-in-drill with oil companies and those Weatherford years, if not the making of Larry Hagman actor, were certainly the making of his creation of J.R. Ewing. He noted all he saw of the Texas oil-rich life. And as he's often expressed, you couldn't put the real Dallas on TV.

When his father made a political bid to become a state senator, the teenage Larry drove him to all his big meetings. 'I met all the dudes down there,' he told Time. 'Oil, cattle, politics, everything. Lemme tell ya, my character of J.R. is milk-toast compared with some of those people. Fratricide, patricide, brothers and sisters shooting each other — it was unbelieveable!'

J.R., he adds, is built up from one of his father's acquaintances — Hagman prefers not to name him. His family probably recognise the portrait, though. Indeed, most families seem to find one of their own kin — or the boss at the office or factory in J.R. Men come up to him in bars and restaurants and say, 'Right on — you're just like my boss / uncle / father / brother.' Then, according to Hagman, the guys leave, and their wives come up. 'Doncha believe him, J.R. — you're just like him!'

It's difficult for a kid to understand ambition in his parents. Larry's mother, as he often points out (or now, he does, he didn't always appreciate the fact) was only 17 years older than he was. By the time he hit his late teens, he began to understand her better. His marriage helped more than anything else, though he also tried the inevitable American route of self-discovery — the analyst's couch.

He's not wailing — and never did — that he had it tougher than any other kids, struggling through adolescence, without much of a goal in sight, other than those offered by divorced parents being obvious successes in their own chosen careers. But being a star's child ain't easy.

There was a period, therefore, when Larry plainly tried to hide from the fact that he was Mary Martin's Son! She invited him to New York where she'd finally made it in Annie Get Your Gun. *He decided to stay put in the real West, and got down to the nitty-gritty of school life.*

By the time he graduated from Weatherford high, he was ripe for a change, however. His mother's graduation present was a trip to Europe. Very good for broadening the soul — and the mind. He spent a couple of months in Sweden — his wife is Swedish, (and perhaps that's why), and he returned home to enrol at Bard College, in Annandale-on-Hudson, in New York.

His mother was still the toast of the town as little Miss Annie Oakley, and the young man could hardly fail but be impressed, and influenced by her triumph. He decided to be an actor! He felt trapped by his decision. He wanted to follow his mother on the stage, but then again he didn't — most of all, he didn't if he was going to be typed as Mary Martin's Son. In this respect, he was luckier than the Fondas and the like. He could keep his true, paternal surname. He could hide from the reality of his celebrity status, although it was that same reality that pushed him on. Double jeopardy!

Hagman's first stage experience was with the Maggo Jones Theatre-in-the-Round in — where else — but Dallas!

He remembers his debut well. It's not the kind of debut one can forget, however much one may want to. He went on stage — opened his mouth . . . and just couldn't spit his one line out.

The second night was better. (It usually is).

Transferring himself again to New York, his mother helped push him into joining the New York City Centre production of Shakespeare's The Taming of the Shrew. *He next bummed around the country in regional theatre and summer stock shows. A drama here, a musical there. Until trying Europe again, joining his mother's new smash hit,* South Pacific, *at London's Drury Lane Theatre. For the princely sum of £12 a week.*

That took care of the next two years until he joined the U.S.A.F. He freely admits to having a good time in blue, and indeed of making sure of such a cushy posting before signing on. His Air Force days were spent in London, in fact, all four years of them. He had time aplenty to produce and direct and act in shows for his fellow servicemen. And to

pull a real J.R. switch on his room-mate — by dating his girl. Maj Axelsson, a Swedish designer.

'She didn't like me very much right away,' he says. 'In fact, not to put too fine a point on it, she thought I was the crassest jerk she'd ever met in her life!'

What woman wouldn't when asked out on a date by this well-heeled, superstar's son in air force blue . . . on a Vespa scooter!

Something sure developed, though. Within a year they were married in 1954, and it's Maj, so he says, who put him straight on most things in life, the role of women, in particular. In short: Maj matured him. She did a helluva job!

After his service days, and still unsure about the acting game, he ran his mother's American ranch for a while, before deciding to have another crack at showbusiness. He tried his luck in several Broadway and off-Broadway plays: Once Around The Block, Career, Comes A Day, A Priest in the House, The Beauty Part. *The titles were often apt for Larry's feelings — once around the block, indeed! — but they weren't much good. Nor was the money.*

The Hagman's had a daughter by now (Heidi — also an actress these days), so he was glad of the regular pay-cheque won from his first brush with soap-opera. He starred in one of them New York day-time TV soaps, still very popular in the United States today, their equivalent of Coronation Street *or* The Archers. *Larry's show was called* The Edge of Night. *He hated it, stuck it out for two and a half years. Good experience, of course.*

He was, then a straight actor, a steady performer, not exactly shining. . . . That began in 1965 when he got his first networked series as Major Anthony Nelson, astronaut, back from space with . . . a girl genie in a bottle. It sounds ridiculous and for those of us who remember it, it was.

By the time it dragged on to its fifth year, Jeannie was less of a dream, more of a nightmare. It became coy, cloying, simply rather asinine. Larry had the bulk of the work to do, the least of the fame or money (and TV stars didn't rate maybe $150,000 a year.

'He had the workhouse part,' is how American TV critic Dwight Whitney put it. 'He was on screen 80% of the time and set up jokes for the star. Barbara Eden breezed into the scene to deliver the

punchline, and he got lost in the shuffle.'

Larry toiled hard in trying to save the show when the magic started to pall. He was forever rewriting the dross-filled scripts. 'I was driven, compulsive. I yelled at people. Finally, I couldn't take it anymore. I started to vomit and it was as if my body were exploding and everything inside were trying to get out . . . including my brain.'

He had the series-disease. Too much repetition, not enough innovation.

Worse still, he found himself typed. In demand, which is not often the case with a star coming from a long-running hit show, but typed! *Mr. Clean. Mr. Straight. Neither of his next two series took off. He was as unhappy with his career as he was blissful with his wife and family (their son, Preson had arrived in 1962). He went back to the analysts' couches, got to know himself, his needs and his ambitions in better order, and started his quite legendary practise of never talking on Sundays.*

'You've got to have a day of rest somewhere along the line,' is how he explains it. 'Every major religion has such a day, right? Well so do I. Don't laugh, you've gotta try it before you laugh at it. You wouldn't believe *how good it is!'*

Larry has maintained his never-on-Sunday talking rule for a decade now. It began by accident. He'd had to shout a lot on a film he was making. Woke up next morning — no voice. He stayed that way on his doctor's advice for a couple of days. 'It was nice,' he grins. And so he made it a rule.

'Oh, sure, it brings a few new problems, but we've licked them all. I'm the one who shuts up, I don't expect the family to do the same. They often do, though. Sundays are very quiet!'

But what about the phone? The smile really lights up. 'That's the real beauty of it,' he says. 'Don't you wish you could spend a day, just one day in seven, where you didn't have to answer the damned phone.'

He does have an emergency phone number available to a limited few people, like his children, mother, agent, or the Dallas *producers. If that phone rings on Sundays, he answers it. He doesn't talk though . . . He whistles.*

Now he's straight-faced (for once). 'Oh shucks, sure, if they're telling me about some real big problems, then I'll talk. Of course, I will.'

Co-starring with Lauren Bacall in the TV version of her Applaus *Broadway musical, helped upgrade the Hagman image. Soon after that, he was busier in films than he had been on the box, and with a greater diversity of roles. The movies include* Stardust *in Britain;* Three in the Cellar; Mother, Jugs and Speed *('Raquel Welch plays Jugs', he guffaws);* Harry and Tonto *with Oscar-winning Art Carney; and two more British films,* The Eagle Has Landed *with Michael Caine . . . and super-Larry even flew into* Superman. *He played the Army major in charge of the missile convoy snatched by Gene Hackman's villain.*

And that was, paradoxically enough, Larry's last movie role before hitting the super-star stratosphere himself as J.R.

By the time he made the first Dallas *tale, he knew television inside out. He's probably guest-starred on every series show there has been in the '70s, and made various tele-flicks —* The President's Mistress *and* Last of the Good Guys, *being among the best.*

He was, then, just about ready for the big time. He'd done time in low dross and high class. He'd settled his head, raised a fine family, and was still madly in love with his wife. 'Why not,' he exclaims. 'Why, I've been married longer than I've done anything else.'

He just never realised what he was letting himself in for when he began choosing stetsons for his new role. Larry Hagman is, without question, the world's most popular TV star. He's too busy to sign autographs, so he gives away specially printed hundred-dollar JR bank-notes. He's now raised it to $1,000 dollar bills. They have J.R.'s face on them.

Working on Dallas *means getting up — and going back to bed — earlier than his fans do. Texas locations are shot first for all the episodes, at the beginning of the production schedule. Once they're in the can, the cast and crew fly back to their homes — and their home from home, the Metro studios.*

Larry Hagman rolls out of bed at 5.30 am — and slides straight into the comforting waters of a jacuzzi bath. His wife designs them, and she came up with a real giant affair for their Malibu home.

Next in the Hagman's routine — because Maj is up with Larry, sharing the jacuzzi — a swift glass of fruit juice, and a run together along the quiet Malibu beach. (Not that quiet; a lot of movie names live in the Malibu colony, and jogging is 'in' for the while).

Back to their pad for some good old English tea, a habit both Larry and Maj acquired during their many years in London, and then he's off to work. Well, he starts work the minute he's into his car and being driven to the studios — he tape-records the day's dialogue, which he had studied, practised and learned the night before.

Inside his studio dressing-room — which didn't look too grand, so he's draped it throughout with flags — he goes over his lines anew. He's being made-up by 7.35 am.

Shooting begins at 8.30.

Apart from interview sessions (and he's talked himself dry with those, so he's cutting them down lately), Larry lunches alone, tucking into a salad he's brought from home. He's been on a vegetarian diet lately.

Then it's all 'Action . . .!' until 7.30 pm at the least.

Not that the day's work is over yet . . . Once back in Malibu, Hagman sets to work on the following day's script, studying the lines, honing them to his oily delivery.

Then he's finished with J.R. for another day. He takes a bath, Japanese style, sloshing buckets of water on him in a small tub, then back into the old jacuzzi with Maj, for champagne and a chat over their day.

A light dinner follows with his wife and their two children — if they're around. Then, bed and sleep by 9.45 pm.

That doesn't even give him time to watch the show. He records it instead, and watches it on his silent Sundays. How even Larry Hagman can view Dallas *without talking — 'That's telling him, boy!', 'Watch yer mouth, Sue Ellen!' — is, quite frankly, beyond us.*

Since the J.R. boom began, he's made one new big film — and it couldn't have a much better title: S.O.B. *His co-stars include Julia Andrews and* Soap *star, Richard Mulligan.*

Larry has plans for more films, via his new production company. Indeed, he's writing one called Vendetta Inc., *which is his way of hitting back at one of the more*

scurrilous American newspapers, which continually misrepresents his (and other top stars') views and quotes and lifestyles.

He's cut an album, has more book and stage offers than he can handle. He's invited to make personal appearances at colleges, supermarkets, clothing stores — and, of course, petrol stations. He's losing weight, that overstuffed look is no more, thanks to a vegetarian diet. His favourite actors are Lord Olivier, Sir Alec Guinness and Robert De Niro — and he has high hopes of his daughter Heidi Hagman's success in this area. He aims to help her all he can. 'I believe in nepotism,' he says. Spoken like a true Ewing.

Life, then, could hardly be better for Larry Hagman. 'I don't have many difficulties,' he nods. 'I've a house, a wife, two wonderful children and enough money for about five years of more. I take all of that very seriously. But I can't take J.R. seriously. If I did that, it would lose its magic.'

No chance of that. Not when he's leapt upon in the street . . . on the beach . . . at premieres . . . or restaurants . . . on planes . . . or on location . . . by women fans of all shapes and sizes. They invariably greet him in exactly the same way.

'I hate you, J.R.,' they say. 'Give me a kiss!'

MISS ELLIE

The Queen Momma

BARBARA BEL GEDDES, real name Barbara Geddes Lewis, is Miss Ellie — Eleanor Southfork Ewing, matriarch of Southfork Ranch, queen-bee in charge of the busiest bees' nest in Texas... no matter what her clan may think!

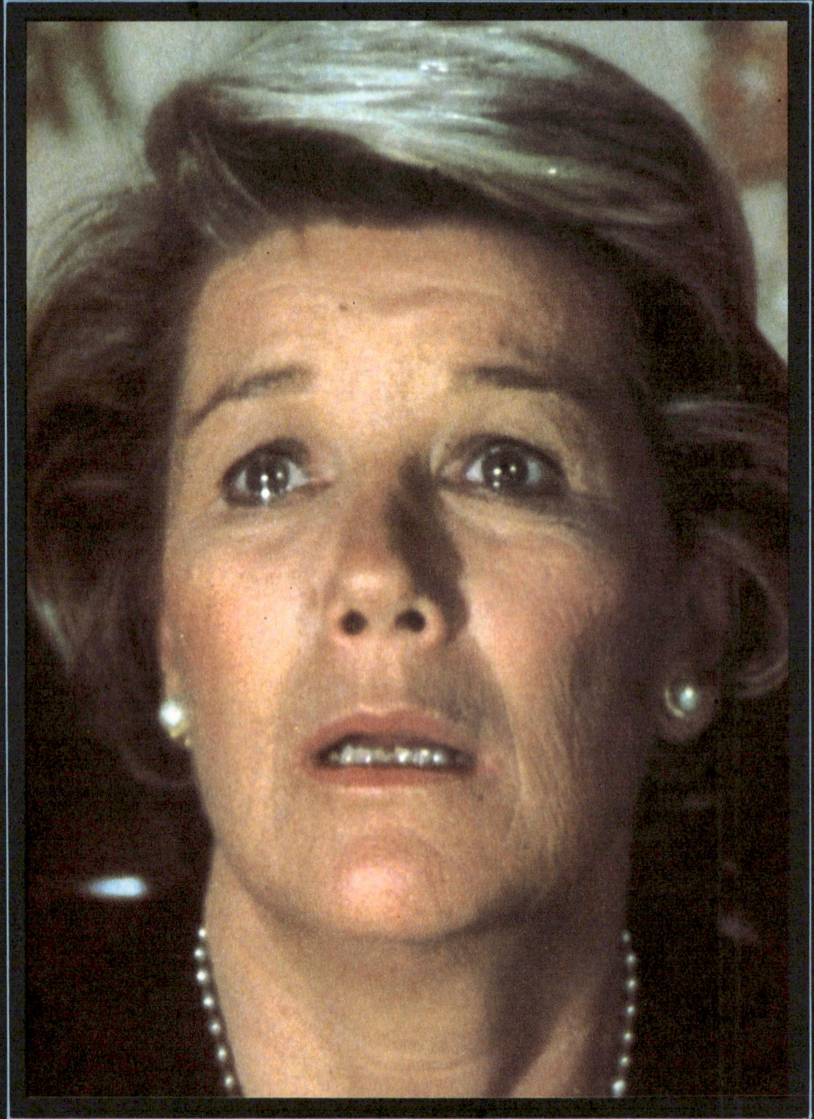

No Barbara... no show! That's the legend around the MGM set of the most popular TV series in the world. If Barbara Bel Geddes a veteran star of stage and screen, had not agreed to come back to Hollywood from her New York home and play Miss Ellie three years ago, *Dallas* would never have happened. Or at least not with today's richly famous cast...

When the first scripts — and feelers — went out to several of the names we know so well today, they just weren't interested in appearing in some weekly soap-opera requiring arduous locations in hot and steamy Texas. Thank you, but no thanks!

Larry Hagman certainly wasn't interested. No way! He'd been along the TV series route before and once (more like thrice) was enough. Besides, he had himself a pretty lucrative thing playing 'real characters' in movies. He was content.

Then, the producers dropped him the news that Barbara Bel Geddes would play Miss Ellie. That changed Hagman's mind... and several others'. 'I don't care how terrible the show is,' he said, 'that lady is somebody I want to act with.' Everyone else said much the same, gladly signed on the dotted line and that's how the Ewings were born. Because Barbara was the big

momma of the Big D.

Of course, if you ask her to confirm any of this, she'll smile shyly and say, 'Nonsense!' She's that kind of lady.

The legend may take some believing in Britain and elsewhere in the world where the Bel Geddes fame was virtually unknown — or just plain forgotten. Apart from people clued up in stage history, she could have been called 'unknown' until her 1978 comeback. In America, though, she has remained a star name of the first magnitude... the Joanne Woodward or Meryl Streep of her day.

Barbara is 59 in October — and she's been an actress since her teenagehood. She made her debut on Broadway in a comedy perhaps aptly called *Out of the Frying Pan*. She was a second from her second Broadway outing. Elia Kazan, the great stage and screen director who, in his time, discovered such greats as Marlon Brando, James Dean, Lee Remick, Paul Newman and Carroll Baker, had noticed Barbara in her comedy and gave her the lead role in the bitterly controversial play, *Deep Are The Roots*. The subject? Inter-racial love. The reviews? Ecstatic. The result? Barbara won the very first Clarence Derwant Award as Outstanding Young Actress of the Year.

From there on, there was nowhere to go but up! And she went! Into films like *The Long Night* (1947) with Henry Fonda, a deft Hollywood re-make of the French classic, *Le jour se leve*... one of the few re-makes considered better than the original. Barbara was outstanding in the old Arletty role.

She next won an Oscar nomination for her top role in *I Remember Mama* in 1948 (since re-staged, and not so well, as a Broadway musical staring Liv Ullmann). Many films followed, including another for Kazan — *Panic in the Streets* with Richard Widmark in 1950 — but Barbara's main love remained the theatre. And Broadway adored her in return. She had the pick of plays and chose some of the most memorable productions of the Great White Way: *The Moon Is Blue*; Graham Greene's *The Living Room*; John Steinbeck's *Burning Bright; Silent Night, Lonely Night; Mary, Mary; Finishing Touches; Luv;* and Edward Albee's *Everything in the Garden*.

Best of all, however, was Barbara's masterly Maggie (the Cat!) in Tennessee Williams' *Cat On A Hot Tin Roof* — directed, again by Elia Kazan. This opened on March 24, 1955, to stunning reviews — and stunned audiences. A tough, hard-hitting play (about a family not unlike a Southern branch of the feuding Ewings) and a great cast: Ben Gazzara, Burl Ives, Mildred Dunnock, Pat Hingle.

Three years later when the movie version was made, only Burl Ives survived. Elizabeth Taylor played Barbara's passionate Maggie.

with Paul Newman in Gazzara's role of her impotent husband. That's Hollywood for you — it takes a long time for the film capital to appreciate greatness...

Not, to be fair, that Hollywood ever forgot Barbara. She was called back to Los Angeles many times and for some very good films. She was a huge hit in the grim *Fourteen Hours* (1951)... shone in Danny Kaye's musical, *The Five Pennies* (1959)... and, of course, was part of Hitchcock's classic *Vertigo* (1958), which is how she won her first most famous TV role...

'Hitch' chose her for the finest of his TV series chillers. Barbara was the murderous housewife in his version of Roald Dahl's wonder-drama with the sting in its tale — *Lamb to the Slaughter*, inspired by Lord Dunsany's *Two Bottles of Relish*. The wife bashes her husband's head in, calls the police saying she's just found his dead body, and then calmly cooks them a meal from the murder weapon — a leg o' lamb!

Ironically, in most current mentions of her previous films, writers forget one that had Barbara in very much a *Dallas* type fix, and even married to a real J.R. type of crud. She played a young girl in *Caught* (1948), close to Sue Ellen and Pam, who believed the only way to happiness was to marry rich!

She did so with a gent name of Smith Ohlrig (yes it was pronounced, would you believe: oil rig), played by Robert Ryan. Wealthy, powerful, scheming, really *evil*, this fella could have taught J.R. a few tricks in business or love affairs. He never liked being beaten in anything. Indeed, he only married the girl because his psychoanalyst (and boy did he need one) said he shouldn't.

By the time Barbara's sweet, if misguided, young thing grew up about life, left him, went to nightschool, learned shorthand and typing, and went to work as the assistant of a doctor working the poor East Side of New York, her quandary was right out of Southfork Ranch. She was in love with the medico (James Mason), but pregnant by the vile Ohlrig. He, of course, agreed to a divorce. On one condition... He must keep the child. Sound familiar?

What's more, Barbara's name in the film was... Leonora. Couldn't be much closer to today's Eleanor, could it?

In between the hard schedule of Miss Ellie's TV life, Barbara Bel Geddes — widow of the late Windsor Lewis — paints and designs greeting cards and stationery for two large American outlets. She inherited these gifts from her famous stage-designer father, Norman Bel Geddes. She has also written and illustrated two children's books: *I Like To Be Me* and *So Do I*. (Pat Duffy has signed copies of both among his large collection of kiddy books and antique toys.)

Once shooting is over for another hectic *Dallas* season, Barbara packs her bags at her Marina del Roy apartment and flies back home to Putnam Valley, in New York State. Not so much to hide away from her renewed fame... but to be close to her daughters, Susan and Betsy, and indeed to her roots. No matter what happens to that brood of hers in Texas, Barbara Bel Geddes is a New Yorker at heart... 'and always will be'.

SUE ELLEN
spouse of a louse!

LINDA GRAY is Sue Ellen, one-time Miss Texas married to Mr. Texas himself, the dreaded J.R.; a nice kind of girl, ruined by a vicious husband, a traumatic marriage, too many affairs, and a son kidnapped within days of his birth . . . little wonder she keeps hitting the bottle.

Whenever she strays far from her Canyon Country ranch at Saugus, Linda Gray, actress, wife, mother, jogger, ski-er, tennis player and raiser of quarter-horses, is always asked the same question. By cops on their 'cycles. By pedestrians at the traffic lights. By headwaiters at the best restaurants. In the beauty parlour or out shopping.

It's the one question that's lasted longer (for her) than who shot what's'name. It's the question we'd all like to ask: How come a great looking chick like you wound up with such a miserable sonuvabitch like J.R.?

Linda doesn't bother anymore to explain that she's married to photographer and art director Ed Thrasher. Or that J.R. is simply a fictional hubby.

By now she has her response off pat. 'Any woman stupid enough to marry J.R. has to have a lot of things wrong with her.'

She worked the answer out for herself soon after starting the series three years ago. That was in the early days when Sue Ellen was not given much to do or say. A 'non-character' as Linda called her.

She started thinking about this poor ex-beauty queen, bought up and owned, like a new side of beef, by her all-powerful husband, and realised the girl must have plenty of flaws, deep down, to have fallen for such an obvious louse. Linda decided to start showing some of the true Sue Ellen, the best way she knew how to. 'I always act with my eyes,' she explains. 'So when it came time for close-ups of each family member, I thought: I'm going to give them a look to kill!'

She did, too.

The producer started jumping when he saw the day's rushes. 'Look at that,' he exclaimed. 'Willya look at that venom in her eyes.' He called up the writers, 'We got to do something

with that part!'

Didn't they just!

The 'sweet young thing' has been turned by J.R.'s less than faithful husbandry into a boozing, two-timing tramp, chasing anything in trousers — Cliff Barnes, Dusty Farlow, and others. Sue Ellen is so muddled now, she's acting as promiscuously as J.R. She doesn't know her past from her Ewings anymore. Doesn't know if she's an alcoholic or not, doesn't know if she loves her son or not.

Only thing Sue Ellen is crystal clear about is that she wants out. J.R., of course, won't let her go. Or not without a fight — which he has got to win.

Linda's eyes are smiling now. . . . She nods, yes, yes, she knows all of this; well, of course she does, she plays the part, she's made the role work. 'Look,' she says, as if you weren't, it's difficult to drag your eyes away from her bright hazel orbs, 'look, if I were in some series where I had to be nice all the time, I'd be so bored!

'Sue Ellen started out that way. I was lovingly referred to by the producer Lenny Katzman as "the brunette on the couch". I mean, I could have been J.R.'s masseuse or something . . .!'

Not any more. Now the eyes have it. They've turned the simple-headed beauty queen into a tortured, agonising soul. They've help turn Dallas into a goldmine. And when they turn on us, turn on him, they depict just how much she loathes J.R. 'Easy,' she says. 'Larry's such a good actor, he's so convincing, I hate him!'

In short, Linda's eyes — and her not inconsiderable acting skills — have turned Sue Ellen around the way she wants her to be. Linda says she loves 'the great broads' of the movies. Stars like Bette Davis and Katharine Hepburn. 'I love crying and letting the mascara run,' she laughs.

She's been along this way before, of course. She made a few years back, a couple of soapy tele-movies, High Rise, and the 1977 return to the scene of the last big soap-opera sensation on the box, Murder In Peyton Place. She knows all about emotional dramatics, then.

A native Californian, like her tele-niece Charlene Tilton, Linda Gray was born by the Pacific at Santa Monica. She attended school right across the street from where she works now for ten, twelve hours a day as Sue Ellen, the MGM studios.

'I used to hang around after school collecting autographs,' she recalls. 'Now it's happening to me.'

Naturally, she never dreamt it would. For she never had any idea about acting for a living. She was far too demure for any such outlandish profession. It was a good Catholic education she received at the Notre Dame Academy, and she was, she freely admits, a very straightlaced young lady after it. 'I swear I was a virgin at 21 when I got married. I just didn't think nice girls went that far. And now . . . I'm doing all kinds of wild, sexy, downright nasty things in front of the entire world. Before I began playing Sue Ellen, I hardly even thought about such things, much less acting them out!'

It was by the sheerest chance that the shy young Linda got into showbusiness. She was sitting in the audience for a fashion show in Los Angeles, when a photographer caught sight of her, offered her his card and suggested she'd make a great model.

She didn't take him seriously. Truth is, she didn't think much about it for some time. 'Girls get this happening all the time in Los Angeles,' she says. 'It was not just me. I didn't think there was anything special about it. It's really a big ploy around here, where guys walk around with cameras. Everybody's a photographer in Los Angeles! Everybody's a star!'

The photographer was serious enough to get in touch with her again. She ran a check on his credentials. He

was legit. No rip-off artist. So, okay, she agreed to some tests.

Well, he was right. She did make a great model. More than 400 television commercials is surely proof enough of that. She enjoyed the work but was still very shy when various people suggested she should move up the ladder and try her hand at movies or television acting. She was wary of such a leap. She'd seen plenty of other models try before her and fall flat on their portfolios.

She knew how to handle cameras — her husband was a photographer after all, an ace at shooting album covers. But Linda was wise enough to realise that working hard for those extra-special, 'give it all you've got, kid' thirty seconds for an advertising spot, hardly compared with the full rigours of rehearsing and acting through an entire film or TV script, with a full cast of supporting and experienced players.

That took tuition. So off she went to acting class, while continuing to model and bring up her two sons: Jeff and Kelly. Knowing the right agents found her in and out of McCloud, Switch and Marcus Welby, MD (she often appeared in the commercial breaks too). She also made one big mistake. Or so she thought. She joined the bizarre soap-opera, All That Glitters. Her role was named after her — Linda Murkland.

Linda G. didn't like the show or the part. Nor did the critics or the ratings. Someone saw it, though, and realised she had what it took to sustain a continuing character in a more dramatic soapie. That's how she married J.R.

Why she's so good at it, she explains best herself. 'I got my big break later than most actresses and I'm making the most of it.'

PRETTY PAM

Bobby's girl

VICTORIA PRINCIPAL is Pamela Ewing, Bobby's wife, whose arrival at Southfork kicked off the series, and the Ewings still aren't too sure about her — being the step-daughter of their oldest foe, with a half-brother ready to ruin them all.

Britain's favourite girl on the Ewing ranch, Victoria Principal, has something of a classic comeback story. One of the innumerable beauties drawn to California by the lure of Hollywood stardom, she came, she saw, she conquered and when things didn't pan out well enough for her — she calmly quit acting and became a show-biz agent.

Dallas is the reason she came back. She's staying this time. And how. 'I'm going to end up as a movie star, a real star after *Dallas* has run its course... in several years.'

Victoria's ups and downs are just another chapter in the story of Hollywood, which often behaves like the biggest spoilt child in the world. It devours whatever it wants and then discards the bones on the rubbish heap. For some inexplicable reasoning, after five good films in three years, Hollywood decided it didn't want Victoria any more.

Instead of bursting into tears, she struck back and said, Okay buster, she didn't want Hollywood either. That hurt! Hollywood didn't like that. Who did she think she was anyway? Well, maybe she thought she was pretty damned good, and maybe she was right. The spoilt child began to have second thoughts. Now that it couldn't have her it wanted her, of course. Just like a child.

Victoria, once bitten, twice shy, decided if she returned it would have to be on her terms. *Dallas* matched those terms and a star is re-born!

'One minute, people are telling you that you are a beautiful desirable young woman,' says Victoria. 'Then, next minute, you can't get a break. You're a has-been... over the hill... after barely getting started in films.

'I did movies with men like Paul Newman and Charlton Heston — and I was still called a starlet! So I left the business and became an agent. And I was a big hit at that.'

It was a slightly masochistic choice of new profession — sending other young hopefuls after the kind of parts she longed to play.

It kept her close to the business, though. She knew everything that was going on. When the old ache to act returned, as she knew it would ('it had never really gone, only the good roles had gone'), she planned her deft come-back. 'I left agenting because people started to think I was flighty or unstable or… something. I wasn't. I'm as ambitious as ever!'

More so than poor Pam Ewing… Bobby also being unfaithful for the first time?

Yes, Pam is a genuine three-handkerchief lady. Nothing but grief since she entered the portals of Southfork. 'Shoot J.R.!' Victoria used to yell back at reporters' questions. 'Of course, Pam was mad enough to shoot him. He made her lose her baby — twice! — thanks to his jealousy and all the angst, anguish and anxiety he caused her.'

heady action in Fukuoko, it's a hamlet near Tokyo, where her Army Air Force Sgt. Major father, Victor Principal was based at the time. (He's of Italian descent; her mother's family stems from England.) By three months old, Victoria was living with her folks in Georgia. By five she was at school in London, 'took me years to lose my British accent'. Next stops included Puerto Rico, Massachusetts, Florida.

Pam Barnes that was, only now she's discovered she's really Pam McKinney, the offspring of 'Digger' Barnes' wife, Rebecca, and her raunchy ranch-hand lover. Pam and Victoria couldn't be more different.

Pam is the poor kid, married very young (a stupid error since annulled), marrying again, slap-bang into the rat-race the Ewings call life. Finding that her father isn't her father… and lord knows where Momma has got to. Added to which, poor, pretty Pam has miscarried two pregnancies, and is now seeing Bobby turning into something of a J.R. as he controls the family business while his brother recovers from a shot in the dark. And isn't

Victoria, on the other hand, has been a globetrotter, jet-setter since birth, living everywhere from Japan to Puerto Rico; attending school in London and Miami; becoming a New York model, girlfriend of the trendy, rich and famous; a Hollywood movie star *and* a nude layout in Playboy…! She surveyed all the rigours the film capital flung at her (well, one film was *Earthquake!*), as well as surviving two serious car-crashes, one robbery at her home, and spare time hobbies such as stockcar racing at 160mph!

Victoria is some high-power lady, and now her motor's really running again.

She was born far away from the

Difficult to settle down to teenage-hood and after, following a hectic start like that.

She also found it difficult to decide on a career. She'd started acting lessons before the family settled in Miami. She continued drama courses there, but entered the Dade Junior College with the idea of becoming a chiropractor — 'in the event I wouldn't make it as an actress'.

Two strings to a bow are always useful. But which one to play? Her first crash smash supplied the answer. Laid up for too long to continue her bone-manipulation studies (and didn't she need them then!), she became an omnivorous

reader, acting out scripts friends brought to her bedside.

She chose her next port of call by herself: New York. Where the best acting action is. Or was... The dying '60s were not the best period on Broadway, not like it had been for Barbara Bel Geddes in the '40s. Victoria (no one calls her Vickie) became a fashion model to help pay for her continued drama lessons. She was called back a second time about the starring role in *Goodbye, Columbus*. Ali McGraw, another model, won the third call — *and* the film.

Fed up, Victoria shot off to Europe, found a new drama mentor from the Royal Academy of Dramatic Art in London, and won her first film role — when British Equity objected because she was American! That decided her. Hollywood must be the place. Studying there with her fifth drama coach, she won another first film — in Manila.

Just before she was due to leave for the location, her agent sent her to meet the great director John Huston — about the role of Paul Newman's Mexican mistress in *The Life and Times of Judge Roy Bean* (1972). Huston liked Victoria, gave her a script and made arrangements to shoot a screen-test next day.

Another girl went to Manila, as Victoria drove to her big test — and had her Jaguar sideswiped by a bus on the freeway! She dashed from hospital to the studios and made the test and won the role — with 40 stitches in her pretty head!

Within days of finally completing that all elusive first film she was offered *The Naked Ape* by Playboy Productions, based on Desmond Morris' British anthropological study. She took her clothes off in the film and for a spread in the magazine — which brought movie offers galore to her door. *Earthquake* with Charlton Heston and Ava Gardner ('she's Capricorn, like me'). Co-starring with Elliott Gould in *I Will, I Will... For Now*. Joining Jan-Michael Vincent's *Vigilante Force*. Being one of the beauty queens kidnapped in *The Night They Stole Miss Beautiful*.

And then, as suddenly as it all started happening — nothing!

Oh, a lot of rubbishy scripts. But she refused to lower her standards, or indeed her principals. She began her new career as a talent agent, and waited. Like Mr. Micawber she just *knew* something would turn up. It did. *Dallas*. And we know the rest of Victoria's hope-opera...

RUGGED RAY
chip off the Jock block

STEVE KANALY is Ray Krebbs, hovering around the series since the start of the Southfork saga, going through as many fights and love-affairs as the rest — and now, suddenly, we find he's Jock's illegitimate son!

Well, come on now, be honest . . . was it really any great surprise? Didn't we really all know it deep inside for the past two years and 53 hours?

I mean, even when they've all got their big white stetsons on, didn't you feel that the ranch-hand Ray Krebbs looked more like big Jock than any of his other sons, J.R., Gary, or Bobby?

And so it has proved to be.

Ray, the brown-haired, blue-eyed wonder boy of the ranch is the result of one of Jock's past love-affairs. Miss Ellie never even guessed it. J.R. certainly didn't — and boy is he mad at the news!

But what else did they think he was roaming around the series for — to be simply background wallpaper? Not Ray. He's one of the few non-Ewings, or financially or legally attached (not to mention romantically), who has been in the Dallas series since it began. So he had to be more important than ranch foreman, huh?

Not only does he look a lot like the Big Daddy of Southfork, he has much the same kind of background as Jim Davis. Although he has made a heap of films — for big and small screens alike — in the last few years, Steve Kanaly doesn't share the same deep down acting roots of the rest of the cast. He's an outsider who broke in . . . just like Jim Davis 40-odd years before him.

Jim was in oil, selling the stuff, when he made the big switch to the movies, and then went to war with the US Navy. Steve was studying art at the University of California, at Northridge (close to where big Jim lives with his Blanche, incidentally) until drafted into the US Army and landed up to his neck in war. Vietnam!

He survived his bitter stint out there with the First Cavalry Division.

He was a radio operator. He prefers television, he'll tell you with a slow, wry smile. Vietnam was no picnic. Apocalypse Now *got it just about right. War is hell. Any war. Back in one piece from 'Nam, Steve returned to a job he used to do while in high school in the San Fernando Valley — managing and instructing riflemen at a trap and skeet shooting club. He also completed his college studies — and makes good use of his art knowledge today as a spare time silversmith.*

Thing was, wherever he went, people always mistook him for a movie star. Or a television star. Or, you know, someone they'd seen someplace . . . A celebrity!

The muddle was understandable. Like his new Poppa, Jim Davis, Steve Kanaly looks the part: a rugged, outdoor, movie star kind of fella. And such folk are, after all, ten a penny around Los Angeles and the San Fernando Valley.

Someone who thought he looked good enough to be in films was one of Francis Coppola's pals, John Milius — the original writer of Apocalypse Now, *in fact. Milius was writing a film in 1972 for John Huston and looking for some new faces to put in it. Unlike Jim Davis' legendary brush with MGM, Milius — a big, bearded guy — wouldn't take 'no' for an answer and fixed Steve up with an audition. He got the part. The film was* The Life and Times of Judge Roy Bean. *There was another newcomer in it, too. Her name was Victoria Principal. (And indeed, years ago, Milius helped another bird to fly into movies in his* Big Wednesday *surfing movie. Her name? Charlene Tilton.)*

John Milius liked how the new kid worked out — and any novice who can survive a film with the legendary John Huston has got to have something between his ears other than pretty blue eyes. So big John put Steve into his own 1973 debut as a director, Dillinger — *and kept a role for him in his next one, too,* The Wind and The Lion *(1975), with Sean Connery. Milius also told another director pal about him and there he was in Steven Spielberg's first cinema movie,* The Sugarland Express *. . . and later on, helping Charlton Heston fight World War II in* Midway.

So that was that!

The fella who happened to look like some movie actor had become some movie actor.

He also popped in and out of TV series — guesting in the major shows of the period like so many other Dallas *newcomers:* Police Story, Police Woman, Rafferty, Hawaii Five-0. *He made a few tele-movies, as well:* Young Joe, The Forgotten Kennedy; Amelia Earhart; Lost; *and* Melvin

Purvis.

Then along came Lorimar Productions with their new adult soap-opera idea dreamed up by writer David Jacobs. A little thing called Dallas. *Okay, why not? He'd never been in a regular series. The money would be useful. He was planning on starting a family — the timing couldn't have been better. And so Ray Krebbs was born. Nine months later, Steve's daughter was born.*

He was there from the first try-out show, Reunion, *on the fringes of it all, like Alan Beam when he arrived. But soon Steve Kanaly had hearts fluttering, fan-mail increasing, and the writers quickly had him fall, head over stetson in love with Susan Howard's Donna Culver . . .*

The real Mrs. Kanaly is called Brent — and they're proud parents of daughter, Quinn Kathryn, now three years old . . . just a handful of months younger than Dallas *itself.*

The Kanalys live in Sherman Oaks, maintaining the outdoor lifestyle both Steve and Ray Krebbs seem to favour. Steve hunts, goes fishing, tends his garden, and tackles the odd set of tennis, and plenty of jogging.

Of course, he has to be careful where he jogs these days. Steve Kanaly has arrived. His face no longer causes him to think they know him — they do! And there's a whole mob around him clamouring for autographs, souvenirs, or just to touch him these days, before you can say Ray Krebbs. He's almost used to it by now. At first, he didn't much like having people 'stand in' for him when the lighting was being arranged for a scene. He definitely objected to the idea of stunt-doubles — preferring to do his own fighting (just as Jim Davis always did). All that, so he thought, was being pampered. And he wasn't used to that — except at home.

Now he appreciates the necessity of such lighting and fighting doubles. Time is money, actors can't do everything, and if he badly injured himself, he could hold up the show. 'Besides,' he nods, 'those guys have got to earn their living as well.'

It's been a helter-skelter ride to the top. Acting for a living, much less becoming a world famous TV star, was the last thing on Steve's mind only a few years back, when he was mending broken skeets. He's no longer working for the rifleman now. He's a big shot!

THE 'SO~YOU~THINK~YOU~KNOW EVERYTHING~ABOUT~DALLAS' QUIZ

There are millions of Dallas *fans out there — somewhere — who can recite everything, chapter and verse, about the world's top tele-series. They know all the trivia. Who's related... in love... or in business with who. Who hates who. They know Barbara Bel Geddes' age, Larry Hagman's mother (well that's easy!). They can name Charlene Tilton's movies, how many Westerns Jim Davis made (which is more than he knows anymore).*

They know how many children Patrick Duffy has, where Larry Hagman lives, the name of Ray Kanaly's wife, and the ages of Linda Gray's two sons. They're positive about where Victoria Principal was born, which musical Larry Hagman appeared in during his London stage days.

*They're pretty sharp on the Ewings, too. Knowing all about Jock's dark past, Miss Ellie's brother, Sue Ellen's lovers, Lucy's affairs, J.R.'s girlfriends and Pam's real parents. They know where Bobby found Gary and where Cliff Barnes works. Why, some of these real ultra-*Dallas *fans even know the name of the show's actual creator... and that does tend to get lost in the publicity shuffle.*

How about you...?

How do you score on Dallas *trivia?*

You are about to find out in this special super quiz, designed in three layers. Easy. Not so easy. And...

What do you do for a living, write Dallas*?*

You begin, of course, at the beginning — and no peeking at the answers yet, or you'll sail through the rest. If you feel you've got through the first section, take a deep breath and proceed to the next bunch of queries — they're harder! If you survive them, you should be confident enough for the real Everest of a test. If you doze off during Dallas*, you won't stand a chance in our grandstand finish. If you stay awake and scrape through this really tough third section, you win the real prize... you get to see the new, fourth series of* Dallas*... oh, any day now, we'd say!*

SECTION ONE: Easy, easy...

1. What is the Ewing's ranch called?

2. Which *Dallas* star was actually born in Texas?

3. Who is the oldest Ewing son?

4. Bobby is married to... who?

5. That was *too* easy... Okay, name Gary Ewing's wife.

6. Until Mary Crosby turned up, who was the youngest star of the show?

7. We know *who*, but how many times was J.R. shot? (Not counting repeats of course).

8. How many wives has Jock had?

9. He came back from the grave, much to Miss Ellie's consternation. Who did?

10. She's Gary's daughter, Jock and Miss Ellie's grand-daughter, J.R. and Bobby's niece, Terry Wogan's fave rave. Her name is...?

11. Who was Pam's step-father?

12. Sue Ellen had a great affair with a cowboy? What's his name?

13. What is Alan Beam's profession: oilman, lawyer, rancher or politician?

14. Pam's brother is now her half-brother. His name's the same. It's what?

15. Who shot J.R.?

See... told you it was real easy. Like all the questions to come — well, er... most of them! — the answers are somewhere in this book. And no, we don't mean on the answers page. No peeking yet, remember, because the questions are getting a mite tougher and only J.R. cheats, right?

SECTION TWO: Think first, okay...?

1. Time for a commercial break. Two of the *Dallas* stars used to be very familiar in American commercials. He sold coffee (well, 'cawfee' he called it); she was a dab hand with hairspray. Can you guess who's who?

2. He thought he was the father of Sue Ellen's baby. Who did?

3. Which of the Ewing actors used to be a stock-car racing driver?

4. Another of the cast also tried racing — in sports cars. Which one?

5. Ray Krebbs fell for her the moment he laid eyes on her in a bar. Who?

6. 'I've finally made it! I'm an 18-year overnight success!' Which Dallaser said that?

7. Miss Ellie has a brother. What's his name?

8. Which *Dallas* star fought in the Vietnam war?

9. He lost everything in J.R.'s Asian oil coup. Who's the actor supplying Vaughn Leland's grim face?

10. Two *Dallas* stars used to headline their own TV science-fiction shows. Name both stars — and their shows.

11. Can you name Pam Ewing's real father?

12. What character is out to ruin the Ewing clan? (Well, which *main* character then, as so many Texans try to bring 'em down).

13. Who originally played Gary Ewing — and who has the role today?

14. What's the name of J.R.'s first secretary?

15. When the snatch went wrong, who was kidnapped instead of J.R.?

Hmm, not really that difficult... perhaps. But you ain't seen nothing yet. Hold on to your hats. Fasten your seat-belts. This is where we separate the Dallas *watchers from the crosseyed* Crossroad *fans. If you can answer all of these final twenty questions, you must be David Jacobs (he's the American who created* Dallas*)... or his wife...*

SECTION THREE: Help!

1. What make of car does Larry Hagman drive?

2. What's the name of Pam's mother?

3. Which *Peyton Place* star once turned up in a *Dallas* yarn?

4. Who plays the mother of Sue Ellen and Kristin?

5. J.R. wanted Lucy to marry him long before Alan Beam showed up with similar ideas. What was his name?

6. Which Ewing was shot before J.R. got his?

7. What is Miss Ellie's maiden name? In full that is: what is Ellie short for?

8. Two Dallas favourites made their film debut opposite Paul Newman in *The Life and Times of Judge Roy Bean*. Which two… and when?

9. The guest-star who took Lucy for a ride later won his own series. Still at the wheel. Name the actor — and his series.

10. Who played J.R.'s first secretary?

11. Two of the cast used to be fans of skeet shooting. He managed a skeet club, she loved the sport. Name 'em both.

12. Who played Donna Culver's husband?

13. She kept coming back for more, Bobby's big romance before Pam. Remember her name?

14. Who first played 'Digger' Barnes?

15. Another *Dallas* guest had J.R. singing her C&W praises. She later headlined her own series. Who was she: Loni Anderson, Penelope Keith, Kate Mulgrew or Pam Dawbar… and name her series.

16. Which *Dallas* beauty entered a Miss Rheingold contest in 1956? Yes, well, the date tends to give it away — so here's the real trivia, what place did she win in the first ten?

17. Film-maker John Milius has been responsible for three of these *Dallas* stars' earliest movies? Name all three — *and* the films!

18. Who is Jock and Miss Ellie's doctor?

19. Who kidnapped J.R.'s baby son?

20. Who shot… no, no, not *him*, even the babies know shedunnit! No, who shot… Jock Ewing?

Answers on page 63

DALLASTROLOGY

Even the stars have stars. They're only human, after all. Some celebrities (notably the late Peter Sellers) take horoscope readings very seriously indeed, and will not make a move — or a movie — unless all is right in their heavens.

When you have as many as a dozen big names in one show, you're bound to hit a double. Or two. Astrologers, we're sure, would make fascinating observations on the very little known fact, until now, that the Virgoes outweigh all the other star signs on the *Dallas* set.

No contest, in fact. Four Virgoes up against a couple of (half-brother) Pisceans . . . and there's no kinship at all between the other six. They're lone stars, suitably enough for a series set in America's lone star state of Texas.

The Virgo quartet make an intriguing bunch. Larry, Linda, Jim and Mary . . . In other words, astrologically speaking, J.R. is a Virgo-son of a Virgo-father, marrying a Virgo-wife . . . and taking her Virgo-sister as his Virgo-mistress.

'Ergo,' chuckles Larry Hagman, 'virgoes have more fun! How much more proof do you need . . .?'

LEO

Keenan Wynn, June 27, 1916.

Interesting how 'Digger' and Cliff Barnes are so close. Leos share more with Arians, though. Affectionate, courageous, ultra-honest and often great intuitive healers. They love to be boss (and then work themselves into cardiac arrests). In a word: attention grabbers. Like Mick Jagger, Peter O'Toole, Robert Mitchum, Robert Culp, Robert Redford (they like Bobs too!). And Mae West was one, which says it all. So was Alfred Hitchcock, which says it again.

VIRGO

Jim Davis, born August 26, 1915.
Linda Gray, September 12, 1944.
Mary Crosby, September 14, 1959.
Larry Hagman, September 21, 1931.

And probably some of the writers, two cameramen, one editor and the tea-lady, as well . . . What a motley crew we have here. Feuding father and son. Feuding sisters. Feuding lovers. Phew!

But that's just their roles. In reality, Virgoes are go-goers. Mad about travel. They're usually rather pious, highly strung people, hard to work with (though this bunch get on fine enough). Rapid learners, paying great attention to the smallest of details. Hard workers then, if shy and reserved. (Larry Hagman, shy and reserved, you've gotta be kidding!) Virgoans often have psychic powers, on top of everything else . . . take your seats please for a Dallas seance. 'Digger, Dusty can you hear us . . .?'

As this quartet have shown, this star sign needs stable marriages for security and roots. They worry, over-fastidiously, about health and special diets, and are never able to relax. One we know of, even does his shopping in a gorilla suit!

SCORPIO

Barbara Bel Geddes, October 31, 1922.

To get technical for once, Scorpio is the eighth zodiac sign, ruled by Mars and influenced by Pluto, and we don't mean Disney's mutt. Strong of will and passions, Scorpions are, alas, greatly prone to jealousy and possessiveness — very suspicious, sceptical people. Fearless, secretive, they're content once they have a clear-cut goal in life. (They make great strikers in soccer!). Barbara's co-Scorpions feature Richard Burton, Rock Hudson, Jodie Foster, Goldie Hawn, Burt Lancaster, Petula Clark . . . and John Cleese.

SAGITTARIUS

Charlene Tilton, born December 1.

Shy about their ages. Well, this one is! Naturally intuitive and indeed philosophical, Sagittarians are excellent survivors. They beat bad health accidents, problems — even pesky uncles! Liberationists, femme or otherwise, they fight like hell for their freedom, to do their thing — and if let alone, they do it well. Affectionate lovers, but not — be warned — easy to live with. One attribute they don't have is tact. Sharing the sign: Frank Sinatra (Mr. Tact himself), Jenny Agutter, Jane Fonda, Sammy Davis, Otto Preminger . . . and Woody Allen.

ARIES

Randolph Powell, born April 14, 1950.

If you get born again, be an Arian. The only star sign worth having. Winners! They have enormous energy and drive, immense charm — when they check their impulsive tempers at the cloakroom. Aggressive individualists all, they have dynamic (if impatient) forces. Leaders among men and women, courageous; love fast cars although accident prone. Steve McQueen was the perfect Arian; his French counterpart Jean-Paul Belmondo continues the bold tradition. Plus Warren Beatty, Julie Christie, Marlon Brando, Spike Milligan and the oldest superstars of all, Mary Pickford and Charlie Chaplin.

Plus Dallas itself, born on CBS TV in America on April 2, 1978!

CANCER

Ken Kercheval, born July 15, 1935.

Eternally young at heart (and they just hate getting older), Cancerians love music and drama, thrive on change — and praise. Without it, they wilt. Thrifty but never mean; reliable, modest, often eccentric and well, damned difficult to understand. They're also great lovers of the past — traditions, antiques . . . even Packard cars, hmm, Ken? Others with the sign: Yul Brynner, Lindsay Wagner, Bill Cosby, Diana Rigg, Karen Black, Ginger Rogers.

PISCES

Steve Kanaly, born March 14.
Patrick Duffy, born March 17.

Yes, shy about their ages. But then Pisces is the most sensitive sign in the Zodiac. They're nice enough, romantic, generous, great party hosts, kind to dumb animals and helping old ladies across the street. Nice folk. Daydreamers, though, often too emotional and sentimental, indecisive and restless for marriage. Though with the mess they make of their homes, they need someone around the joint. Ask Lee Marvin, Bruce Forsythe, Rudolf Nureyev, Joanne Woodward, or Liz Taylor!

CAPRICORN

Victoria Principal, born January 3, 1950.

Capricornians are strong, healthy, long livers, thrifty, (very economical), selfish, arrogant, dominant, sulky, vindictive, slow to burn with anger, slower still to forgive and forget — and usually prepared to make any sacrifice in the name of personal ambition. Recognise much of Victoria there — or Ava Gardner, Susannah York, Anthony Hopkins, Jon Voight?

'DIGGER'S' SON
sworn to ruin the Ewings

KEN KERCHEVAL is Cliff Barnes, 'Digger's' son, Pam's half-brother, determined to bring the Ewings to heel, expose their frauds, ruin their power and destroy them all . . . including Pam?

When 'Digger' Barnes died, he revealed one big secret — and let his old foe Jock Ewing off a murder charge hook. But 'Digger' took a lot more secrets with him. They will all be revealed, though. His son, Cliff, has them now and is building on them all the time for his constant attacks on the Ewings who he feels — and perhaps quite rightly — destroyed his venerable old boozehound of a pappy.

'Digger' is the sole member of the original Dallas *cast to have died. (Or he is, as we write this . . .) But his ghost goes marching on, haunting the series . . . feud for thought, in search of vengeance.*

Cliff is his instrument. Southfork is his target and all who live in it. Jock for 'cheating' him. Miss Ellie for 'jilting' him. And the rest of the Ewing zoo for well, simply being Ewings, that'll do!

Southfork is still 'Digger's' target for destruction — and all who live in it. Cliff is his instrument, his avenging angel.

It hasn't happened yet, but it could . . . any day now. Cliff Barnes winning this age-old struggle and suddenly breaking out in song. 'If I Were A Rich Man . . .'

Ken Kercheval would love the irony of that. A double irony. Cliff Barnes, of course, wants to be as big as the Ewings. 'No,' says Ken, 'bigger . . . richer!' And Ken, powerhouse actor, is underneath it all, a frustrated singer.

He's appeared in all the big stage musicals, Fiddler on the Roof, Cabaret *and* The Apple Tree. *He majored in music and arts at the University of Indiana. All the shows he performed in there — likewise at the Pacific University at Stockton, California, and the Neighbourhood Playhouse in New York — were musicals.*

Ken has a great voice — well loved and remembered back home in Clinton, Indiana. It's just that he suddenly won more fame as a straight actor, so he hasn't much time for exercising the old larynx anymore. 'Except in the shower'. Don't be too surprised, though, if a Singalong Ken Kercheval *album is in the record shops before too long. He'd love it — and wouldn't his* Dallas *fans be taken aback?*

What's that? But, of course, he has *fans! The Ewings, let's be frank, are hardly the most admirable family in town. In any town! They're mean, avaricious, sly, underhand, crooked, mendacious . . . pretty rotten to the core. Well, all except Miss Ellie . . . and some of us are not too sure about her real past!*

Cliff Barnes, therefore, is the one true hero of the series. If J.R. is merely taking care of the business, Cliff is trying to take care of the law — and slap the Ewings inside. If only he could get all his facts right one day, tie up all the evidence he needs, have one of the brood turn traitor and blow the whistle, why then he could bring them all to their knees.

And then, wouldn't we holler with delight!

Or would we?

Half the reason we all wanted to know who shot J.R. is because we knew he wasn't killed, and could anticipate how he'd get even with his sniper? Half the reason we all enjoy Cliff's efforts to get the goods on J.R., is because we know he'll wriggle out of it somehow, pass the buck to some poor sucker, or quite simply buy the judge.

Maybe the real success of the series, therefore, is that such a vile brood does get away with all it gets away with! We enjoy their money-talks machinations — yet we also feel that Cliff Barnes, like Kojak *and* Columbo*, must win in the end . . . and wind up king of Southfork.*

He's the underdog, and the British, more than most, always root for the underdog. For, remember, every underdog has his day. Cliff deserves it. He's really been trying. 'Yeah,' J.R. would sneer 'very trying!'

Cliff is now learning to bide his time. He's shot his bolt too often in the past. The Senator Orloff affair, for instance, blew up in his face. And when J.R.'s bank loan was due, and Cliff was still head of the Office of Land Management and able to turn the screw, Miss Ellie came to Southfork's rescue.

Cliff's greatest hour was ruined closer to home — by his father 'Digger'. There was Cliff, a new assistant district attorney, dragging up the 28-year-old murder case of the body found on the Southfork ranges . . . and having Jock arrested, charged and indicted in court for the murder of his ranch-hand, Hutch McKinney.

Alas poor Cliff. 'Twas his father whodunnit! 'Digger' Barnes confessed all to Miss Ellie as he died. It was, of course, a killing for all the usual Dallas*-convoluted reasons. Hutch McKinney was about to run off with 'Digger's' wife, Rebecca. She was pregnant at the time — with McKinney's child. Pam Ewing, née Barnes, was suddenly née McKinney! At least that solved Pam's worry about inheriting 'Digger's' terrible genetic disease.*

But Cliff's moment of glory went up in smoke (again). He lost his case. He lost his sister. Though, of course, like old 'Digger' who had disowned her, Cliff already felt Pam a lost cause by marrying into the Ewings in the first place.

The bitter feud between the two families goes way, but way back, to when Jock and 'Digger' were young oil workers — sudden partners in a rich field of their own. They split when Jock used his larger share of their loot to sweet-talk (some say, buy) 'Digger's' girl into marriage — Miss Ellie.

Because of their feud, there were many people who backed Cliff heavily in the big gambling on who shot J.R. What nonsense. Cliff may be mean — and he's getting meaner, more neurotic every episode — but he wouldn't resort to killing the man. He simply wants to see J.R. crawl . . . and to wipe that smirk off his chops.

So you have to give old Cliff his due — just like Sylvester the Cat, he never *gives up the fight.*

Following his rich career on Broadway — he tackled some dramas there as well as musicals — Ken Kercheval hit the movie capital with a bunch of fine films. He was in Pretty Poison*, a murder thriller with Anthony Perkins and Tuesday Weld in a role quite similar to sultry Lucy Ewing. Ken also appeared in Roy Schneider's cop drama,* The Seven Ups *. . . in* Network *with the late Peter Finch, and in Sylvester Stallone's trades union expose,* F.I.S.T.

His earlier Hollywood days also traversed the inevitable guest-star route into TV — all the way from Telly Savalas' Kojak *to Patrick McGoohan's rapidly axed* Rafferty*. Ken also starred in* The Coming Assunder of Jimmy Bright *and such tele-flicks as* The Scottsboro Boys *and* Separating.

Dividing his time between Los Angeles and New York — and, naturally, his location forays into Dallas itself — Ken has two sons, Aaron, 24, and Caleb, 19, and a daughter of 21 called Liza. Apart from this family, his spare time is spent in pursuits not quite as athletic as some of the Dallas *cast — but just as expensive.*

Like Larry Hagman, Ken is an avid collector. Larry goes in for hats and flags and stuff. Ken has this passion for early American glasswork . . . regional painters of the 1930s . . . and the most expensive toy of all, Packard cars. He buys them in most any condition and spends a fortune on restoring them by himself. So far, he has two 1941 Packards — a coupé and a convertible — in excellent shape. Or they are now that he's finished working on them.

'I'd like more,' says Ken. 'I'm always interested. The problem is finding the garage space.' Maybe that's what he wants to run the Ewings off Southfork for. . .

When 'Digger' Barnes first showed up on the Ewing spread, in the first chapter of Dallas *— right after Bobby's surprise marriage to 'Digger's' daughter, Pam; he was played by David Wayne, the wry character actor from such films as Marilyn Monroe's* How To Marry A Millionaire *and Joanne Woodward's 1957 Oscar-winner,* The Three Faces of Eve*. Wayne's version of 'Digger' stuck around for a few episodes, full of hate for the Ewings and then quit Texas in a huff. There was now way he could break them!*

When the character came back for a new outing — a new gloating over his son's success, in romancing Sue Ellen away from J.R. — Keenan Wynn had taken over the role for the second full series.

HOW MUCH OF L.H. IS THERE IN J.R. ?

To most of the free world Larry Hagman and J. R. Ewing are one and the same person. People hail the actor as J.R. with a few expletives deleted for their adjectives. He plays up the part in his chat-show appearances, publicity tours — even on his record album.

Does he know where one begins and the other leaves off?

'Oh shucks, sure I do,' he replies with a merry twinkle in his suitable green-as-envy eyes. 'I know enough of J.R. to know what *he* is and what I am. I mean, hell, he's rotten, right? Absolutely rotten.

'And me, well, I'm kinda lovable wouldn't you say?'

A pause. 'I love him, too, you know. I mean he is some great character. Don't know if I'd invite him to my house, but he's okay.

'And it's fun — hell, it's great fun! — being the bad guy for once. I've played too many good guys. But J.R. is really no worse than the rest of the Ewings.

'I just try to give him that little something extra, know what I mean. A kinda joyful quality in my raping, pillaging, murdering. He speaks soft. He smiles just before he gets ya! Oh, he's getting more devious all the time.'

According to the way Larry Hagman reads it, J.R. is even a good family man, as well. . . .

He certainly doesn't quite measure up to Larry in that respect. Hagman's had but the one big love affair in his life. (And no, we don't mean with himself). With his wife, Maj.

J.R., according to Time's TV critic Richard Corliss, 'struts, whinnies, talks out loud to himself; he has a grand time being bad. His soft, smooth, surprisingly characterless expresses J.R.'s childishness; but those huge blue eyes testify to ages of suffering given and received.'

Larry Hagman doesn't fit that portrait at all. Or not any more.

He's had his helping of suffering, as a kid torn between divorced parents, as an actor trying to make it on his own talent and not just because he was Mary Martin's lad. But he laid all that to waste years before *Dallas* came along. He just draws on it now — some of it.

J.R.'s humour is rather sick — it involves ruining his business associates, turning his wife into a drunk, making life in Texas so much of a hell for Gary that he quit — and Bobby keeps on leaving.

Larry's humour is just . . . well, plain whacky, most of it. He's been known to turn up on the set with instead of his stetson, a fireman's helmet on. . . . He has a thing about a gorilla suit. He loves to wear one when out driving his car. Other drivers are shattered by the view!

Dressing up is the hallmark of his fun and games.

When J.R. smiles, he smiles mean. When Larry smiles, he's usually bursting into laughter.

The difference between the two men — the fact and the fiction — can best be summed up in the stern look that was always on John Paul Getty's face when he was alive and the richest man in the world . . . and looked so miserable about it.

J.R. was born rich and is scared stiff of losing it, wanting only to amass more and more greenbacks, *and* oil wells *and* banks. For the family, or so he says, the liar.

Larry Hagman was born pretty well-off, fair to middling. What he's got today, is what he worked for. And he's aiming to enjoy it.

L.H. love life.

J.R. keeps fighting at it.

THE EARLY YEARS

Time to spin back the clock, and take a look at what brought the Ewings to where they are today — the most famous American family since the Kennedys. It started, but of course, as it went on. With the family grouped together, smiling broadly — and at each other's throats.

Okay, all aboard the Dallas time-capsule, back to . . .

1978
Episode 1:
DIGGER'S DAUGHTER

Bobby Ewing, youngster of the oil and cattle dynasty, shakes the clan by coming home with a bride: Pamela, daughter of Jock Ewing's arch enemy, 'Digger' Barnes. Bobby demands a more vital role in the family business which wipes the deadly smile off J.R.'s chops. He views Bobby as a new threat to his own ambitions, and Pam as a spy for her father and brother, Cliff. *[Director, Britain's Robert Day. Guests, David Wayne as 'Digger'; Tina Louise as J.R.'s secretary, Julie Grey . . . remember her?]*

2. THE LESSON.

Pam attempts to convince Bobby's niece, Lucy, to stay in school — and out of trouble. No way! Lucy forces the issues by faking an assault by her student counsellor. *[Director, Irving J. Moore]*.

3. SPY IN THE HOUSE.

Cliff Barnes has a document linking Senator Orloff in a shady finance deal with the Ewings. J.R. accuses Pam of supplying the evidence. Only Bobby believes her innocence and shifts them both out of Southfork. J.R. smiles. *[Director, Robert Day. Guest, Norman Alden as Sen. Orloff]*.

4. WINDS OF VENGEANCE.

Hurricane at Southfork. Inside and out. J.R. and Ray Krebbs, the only men around, are forced into a corner when heavies Luther Frick and Payton Allen arrive hell-bent on revenge . . . Luther suspects J.R. of playing around with his wife. *[Director, Irving J. Moore. Guests, Brian Dennehy, Cooper Huckabee as Luther and Payton]*.

5. BARBECUE.

Pam is pregnant! She hopes the good news will finally unite the warring grandpas-to-be, Jock and Digger. Think again, kid. *[Director, Robert Day]*.

1978/9
6. REUNION (two-parter).

Bobby brings his missing brother, Gary, home from Las Vegas. 'Tis a chilly reunion. J.R. feels Gary will dilute his power-base, and fights hard, in his own ever-smiling manner, by pressuring Gary into taking over one of the Ewing combines. Gary's ex-wife, Valene — also brought home by daughter Lucy — smells a rat in J.R.'s plans. Digger Barnes, drunk again, disowns Pam for marrying into the Ewings. *[Director, Irving J. Moore. Guests, David Ackroyd as Gary; Joan Van Ark as Val]*.

7. OLD ACQUAINTANCE.

Bobby's old flame, Jenna Wade, turns up seeking aid for her fatherless daughter, 'Charlie'. Fearing the child could be his, Bobby helps Jenna more than he should or so Pam thinks. *[Director, Alex March. Guest, Morgan Fairchild as Jenna]*.

8. BYPASS.

Jock has a heart attack. J.R.'s fault! Or Bobby's renewed threat to quit Ewing Oil due to J.R.'s business tactics. He's not wrong . . . As Jock has open-heart surgery, J.R. is making deals on the possibility of his father's death. *[Director, Corey Allen]*.

9. BLACK MARKET BABY

Determined to beat Bobby and Pam to producing the first Ewing grand-child, J.R.'s wife, Sue Ellen, resorts to black-market adoption — hoping to buy Rita's unwanted baby. *[Director, Larry Dobkin. Guest, Talia Balsam as Rita]*.

10. DOUBLE WEDDING

J.R. is all smiles when visited by Ed Haynes, who says he's Pam's first husband and wants her back! Well, yes, Bobby, she'd kept her first marriage secret. Just one of those teenage lapses, long since annulled. Except to J.R.'s glee, she's lost the papers which prove she's not a bigamist. *[Director, Paul Stanley. Guest, Robin Clarke as Haynes]*.

11. RUNAWAY

Happy birthday, Lucy! Not really. Jock refuses to invite her mother to the clambake. So Lucy splits, hitches a ride from Willie Guest . . . a psychotic thief in search of a new Bonnie and Clyde-like pardner. *[Director, Barry Crane. Guest, Greg Evian as Willie]*.

12. ELECTION

Cliff Barnes stands for state senator. Pam defiantly supports her brother against the Ewing candidate. She also talks too much and J.R. (who else?) hears enough to smear Cliff and ruin his trust in Pam. *[Director, Barry Crane]*.

13. SURVIVAL

J.R. and Bobby's plane crashes in a swamp during a thunderstorm. The Ewing women keep the news from Jock, recovering from his heart operation. They wait and pray and reveal more of their personalities and feelings about their men. *[Director, Irving J. Moore]*.

14. ACT OF LOVE

While J.R.'s away, Sue Ellen plays with Cliff Barnes. She then surprises everyone, herself and J.R. included, by learning she's finally pregnant after seven years marriage. *[Director, Corey Allen]*.

15. TRIANGLE

Ray Krebbs — and J.R. — fall for ambitious C&W songthrush, Garnett McGee. Ray proposes marriage; J.R. proposes money — to get Ray out of the way and far from Southfork. *[Director, Vincent McEveety. Guest, Kate Mulgrew as Garnett)*.

16. FALLEN IDOL
Bobby paints the town red with his old college idol, 'Guzzler' Bennett. They plan to go into the construction business, building a huge shopping centre. Not on the Southfork range you don't says, Miss Ellie — and J.R. *[Director, Vincent McEveety. Guest, Richard Kelton as 'Guzzler']*.

17. KIDNAPPED
Three hoods grab J.R. for a $1,500,000 ransom. They snatch the wrong target — Bobby! Cliff Barnes is their go-between until J.R. handles the deal his way. *[Director, Larry Dobkin. Guests, Paul Koslo, Kelly Jean Peters, Stephen Davies as the hoods]*.

18. HOME AGAIN
Miss Ellie's brother, Garrison, turns up — back from the 'dead'. And the ever-righteous Ellie wants to give him back his true inheritance — Southfork Ranch. Few Ewings agree. *[Director, Don McDouglas. Guest, Gene Evans as Garrison Southworth]*.

19. FOR LOVE OR MONEY
Tired of J.R.'s pecadilloes, Sue Ellen plans to leave him for Cliff Barnes? Her mother and sister back her up — useless against J.R.'s cunning. *[Director, Irving J. Moore. Guests, Martha Scott as Mrs. Shepard; Colleen Camp as Kristin)*.

20. JULIE'S RETURN
Okay, do you remember her now? Julie Grey returns to town and Jock seem's highly smitten — tired of being treated as an invalid by the family. J.R. tells Miss Ellie all. *[Director, Les Martinson. Guest, Tina Louise as Julie]*.

21. THE RED FILE (two-parter)
Now it's Julie fed up with J.R. So she spills many of his business secrets to Cliff Barnes. But when Julie goes missing, J.R. neatly frames Cliff for her murder. Pam (Cliff's sister, remember?) leaves Southfork in anger, putting Bobby in a huge quandary. He has evidence to free Cliff, but also too much about J.R.'s illegal activities. *[Director, the show's producer Leonard Katzman]*.

22. SUE ELLEN'S SISTER
Now that Pam's long gone, Sue Ellen's sister, Kristin Shepard, makes a play for Bobby — encouraged by J.R. Cliff uses Pam to slow down a Ewing Oil deal which doesn't help the young couple any. *[Director, Irving J. Moore. Guest, Colleen Camp as Kristin]*.

23. CALL GIRL
Pam's new chum, Leanne, has a past shady enough for J.R. to blackmail her into killing two birds (Pam and her brother's big-wheel backer) with one hidden photographer. *[Director, Les Martinson. Guests, Veronica Hamel as Leanne; Fred Beir as Maxwell Benson]*.

24. ROYAL MARRIAGE
Lucy's in love! J.R.'s tickled pink! But he's not interested in marrying Kit Mainwairing III to unite the biggest oil families into a mammoth Texas combine with J.R. at the top. *[Director, Gunnar Hellström. Guests, Mark Wheeler as Kit; Linden Chiles, Jay W. MacIntosh as his folks]*.

25. THE OUTSIDER
This love bug sure am catching . . .! Ray Krebbs falls for Donna, not knowing she's wed to powerful Sam McCullum — dealing with J.R. to squelch Cliff's harassment of Ewing Oil. *[Director, Dennis Donnelly. Guests, Susan Howard as Donna; John McIntire as McCullum]*.

26. JOHN EWING III (two-parter)
Drugs at Southfork. Sue Ellen's on the bottle, Lucy's on pills. J.R. plonks his wife in a sanitorium and takes great glee in showing her evidence of Cliff's new girl. Great atmosphere for J.R. Jnr's birth! *[Director, Leonard Katzman]*.

1979/80
27. WHATEVER HAPPENED TO BABY JOHN? (two-parter)
The kid is soon used to such goings on. While he's still in hospital, Sue Ellen doesn't seem to care about him, Cliff Barnes claims him as his own son.

28. THE SILENT KILLER
Cliff shows off to Dad how he's getting even with them Ewings but 'Digger' Barnes' illness ruins his joy. The old-timer has the same genetic complaint as *The Elephant Man*. It's hereditary. So his kids, Pam and Cliff have it, so will *their* kids — and Cliff is sure J.R. Jnr. is his child! *[Director, Irving J. Moore. Guest, Keenan Wynne as the new 'Digger' Barnes. New to the series: Mary Crosby as Sue-Ellen's sister, Kristin Shepard . . . aha!]*.

29. SECRETS
Lucy's Ma tries to re-establish some contact. Small-fry drama compared with Pam finding she's pregnant (again?), and hiding the news — and her family's genetic history — from Bobby. *[Director, Leonard Katzman. Guest, Joan Van Ark as Valene Ewing]*.

30. THE DOVE HUNT
Jock's shot! J.R. gets hit, too, by sniper's bullets while they're out hunting. Bobby and Ray have to leg it for help. Thinking he's dying, Jock reveals a secret to J.R., something he's kept from Ellie all these years. He'd been married before. Wow! *[Director, Leonard Katzman. Guest, Robert J. Wilke as the sniper Tom Owens]*.

31. THE KRISTIN AFFAIR
Having failed with Bobby last year, Kristin chases after J.R. Bobby discovers Pam's pregnancy before she can decide on a secret abortion. *[Director, Irving J. Moore]*.

32. THE LOST CHILD
Proud father-to-be Bobby grows fond of one of the ranch-hand's kids, and so Pam reveals the dangers to their expected child. J.R. sets a private eye on Sue Ellen's frequent forays into town. *[Director, Irving J. Moore]*.

33. RODEO
We've never seen it before, but the Ewings sponsor a rodeo every year. They won't forget this one. Sue Ellen falls for one of the cowboys, Dusty Farlow. *[Director, Leonard Katzman. Guest, Jared Martin as Dusty]*.

34. MASTECTOMY (two-parter)
Miss Ellie has a lump in her breast and requires a mastectomy operation. She can cope with that, but how will Jock react? He's told her now how he left his first wife when she became mentally ill. Will he walk out on her, too? No way.

He's as much in love with Ellie . . . as Sue Ellen seems to be with Dusty. *[Director, Irving J. Moore].*

35. ELLIE SAVES THE DAY

J.R.'s in the mire. . . . Typhoons delay drilling in his Asian fields. His bank loan is due. So he simply mortgages Southfork! Bobby tells Jock and Ellie they could lose their home. Ellie gives in. J.R. can also drill for oil on her ranchland. *[Director, Gunnar Hellström].*

36. MOTHER OF THE YEAR

Sue Ellen still avoids her baby like the plague causing rows with J.R.; Bobby and Pam, too, who look upon John Jnr. as their own. (Somebody has to). Ellie's so upset by the oil work at Southfork, Jock decides to sell up in Asia. J.R. fights against losing such millions. *[Director, Larry Hagman. Guests included Joycelyn Brando, Marlon's sister].*

37. RETURN ENGAGEMENT

Lucy's father Gary Ewing, is back in town, re-marrying Lucy's mother, his ex-wife Valene, before moving to California (well hello *Knots Landing!*). Sue Ellen tells Kristin's boyfriend, Rudy, where she is — on a business trip with J.R., where else? *[Director, Gunnar Hellström. Guests, Ted Shackelford as the new Gary; Joan Van Ark as Valene; Terry Lester as Rudy].*

38. LOVE AND MARRIAGE

J.R. figures the best way to keep Jock out of the office is bringing Bobby back into Ewing Oil. Pam using her own work to hide her own problems. Ray Krebbs is happier — Donna Culver (ex-McCullum) is back in his life. *[Director, Alex Singer. Guests, Susan Howard as Donna; Mel Ferrer as Harrison Page].*

39. POWER PLAY

Kristin blows the whistle on Lucy's affair with Alan Beam. But instead of chasing off the power-hungry lawyer, J.R. encourages his wedding plans. Lucy has other ideas. *[Director, Leslie Martinson. Guests, Susan Howard, Keenan Wynn].*

40. PATERNITY SUIT

So who *is* J.R. Jnr.'s dad? Digger tells the Press it's Cliff. Jock sues. Cliff Barnes sues back, for custody of 'his' child. Sue Ellen, J.R. and Cliff take blood tests . . . and J.R. finally embraces *his* son. *[Director, Harry Harris. Guests, Keenan Wynn; Jared Martin as Dusty].*

41. JENNA'S RETURN

Oh what a tangled web of love . . . Sue Ellen still sees Dusty. Pam walks out on Bobby. Ray questions his affair with Donna. Bobby runs again into old flame Jenna. And Kristin takes advantage of J.R.'s anger (jealousy?) with Sue Ellen. *[Director, Irving J. Moore. Guests, Francine Tucker as the new Jenna; Mel Ferrer, Jared Martin].*

42. SUE ELLEN'S CHOICE

The tangles continue . . . pressured by Dusty, Sue Ellen asks J.R. for a divorce. Jenna visits Pam to declare her intentions about Bobby. Donna makes a final attempt to persuade Ray to marry her. *[Director, Leonard Katzman].*

43. SECOND THOUGHTS

J.R. still pushing Alan Beam into marrying Lucy — and move to Chicago. But Jock gets the lawyer a new partnership deal in Dallas. Kristin finds out about Alan's other girlfriend, but Lucy announces a wedding date anyway. *[Director, Irving J. Moore. Guest, Keenan Wynn].*

44. DIVORCE — EWING STYLE

Preparing for her divorce, Sue Ellen becomes the perfect wife and mother — and sticks a private eye on J.R.'s nocturnal trysts with Kristin. J.R. hits back, determined to stop his wife leaving him with their child, by proving she's drinking again. *[Director, Leonard Katzman].*

45. JOCK'S TRIAL

Now she *is* boozing — following Dusty's death in a plane crash. Instead of a divorce case, though, we have a murder trial. New assistant D.A. Cliff Barnes digs up the old mystery of a body found at Southfork and indicates Jock for murder. Top attorney Scotty Demarest fears Jock's chances (particularly with J.R.'s evidence), but poor Cliff is thwarted. On his deathbed, 'Digger' Barnes confessed to Miss Ellie that . . . hedunnit! Because his wife was running off with the victim, Pam's true father! *[Director, Irving J. Moore. Guests, Keenan Wynn's farewell as 'Digger'; Stephen Elliott as Demarest; William Watson as the victim, Hutch McKinney].*

46. WHEELER DEALER

While the clan's away (visiting Jock's first wife, Amanda in a Colorado sanitorium), J.R. plays Monopoly with the tip that their Asian oilfields are about to be nationalised by the new regime. Pam, meantime, starts looking for her mother. Sue Ellen? Hitting the bottle again. *[Director, Alex Singer. Guest, Lesley Woods as Amanda Ewing].*

47. HOUSE DIVIDED

Quaint title for the J.R. Gets His episode. . . . His coup in selling off the Asian oil leases before the nationalisation news hits the headlines, wipes out all the buyers overnight. J.R. lies in his smiling teeth that he knew this would happen. Bobby's so disgusted, he quits Southfork with Pam — again! Sue Ellen quits drinking to squash J.R.'s efforts to pack her off to the tank — again! Cliff Barnes plans revenge — again! Then somebody — Bobby, Sue Ellen, Kristin, Jock, Miss Ellie, Alan Beam, Vaughn Leland, or even Dusty and Digger back from the grave? — pumps J.R. full of lead. *[Director, Irving J. Moore].*

1980/81

Aw c'mon — you know what happened from thereon . . . The burning question now is what happens in the fourth series. Will Bobby's top job turn him into a new J.R.! Will one of Pam's pregnancies ever bear fruit? How many secrets does Miss Ellie really know? Is Jock really a Ewing anyway? Can Ray Krebbs stop J.R. smiling — please? Why did that student *really* marry Lucy? Is Dallas big enough for J.R. or are his sinister eyes really set on Washington? J.R. For President was a joke last year, but then so was Ronald Reagan. Think about it. Isn't it about time somebody moved out of the overcrowded Southfork, so why not J.R. in the White House?

It's easy to joke about the possibilities. Just don't laugh too loud. They'll probably all happen.